Love Letters in Poetic Verse

A poetic anthology
celebrating love and relationships

Paul Gilliland

Editor-in-Chief

Southern Arizona Press

Southern Arizona Press

The mission of Southern Arizona Press is to promote the works of self-published and lesser-known unpublished authors and poets to the rest of the world through publishing themed and unthemed anthologies and assisting in the publication and promotion of their works.

It is our desire to make the voices of these aspiring poets and authors available to as wide an audience as possible with the belief that no writer of poetry or literature should ever have to pay to have their works published.

Love Letters in Poetic Verse

All rights reserved. Copyright © 2023 by Paul Gilliland and Southern Arizona Press. Except as permitted under the Copyright Act of 1976, no portion of this book may be reproduced or distributed in any form, or by any means without prior written consent of the individual authors or the publisher. Individual works Copyright © retained by the poetic author. Previously published works have been cited and each publication acknowledged to the best of our ability. If any citations have been missed, such errors will be corrected in subsequent reprints.

If you would like your work to be considered for future anthologies, please visit us at http://www.southernarizonapress.com/current-submissions/ for a full list of current open anthology submissions and submission guidelines.

Published by Southern Arizona Press
Sierra Vista, Arizona 85635
www.southernarizonapress.com

Follow us on Facebook at:
https://www.facebook.com/SouthernArizonaPress

Format, cover design, and edits by Paul Gilliland, Editor-in-Chief, Southern Arizona Press

Cover Art: *Romeo and Juliet* by Frank Bernard Dicksee, 1884

Poets photos Copyright © retained by submitting poets

ISBN: 9781960038074

Table of Contents

Linda M. Crate   16

> wildflowers
> this is our kingdom
> shine and bloom
> true love never dies
> this love of mine
> you are the sun and i am your moon

Michael Thomas Ellis   23

> Purr
> A Short Tribute to the Word Quiver
> A Thousand Pebbles
> Soft Parade of Sighs
> Leonid
> Sunrise Sunset

James Thomas Fletcher   42

> Postcard from Now
> Appariation
> Quantum Entanglement
> Star-Quaker
> Spelunking the Past
> The Third Solar Cycle

Swayam Prashant   52

> Will You Be My Valentine
> An Open-eyed Dream
> Thirst Alive
> Arch Beauty
> A Century of Love

Eduard Schmidt-Zorner   58

>*Found You*
>*For Baroness M.*
>*Your Hand in Mine*
>*Croatian Memories*
>*Notes of Times Gone By*

Jamie Santomasso   66

>*Ode to the Fire*
>*Galaxy's Billet-doux*
>*i'll carry your heart*
>*Wilted Rose*
>*She*

Rp Verlaine   74

>*Beginnings*
>*Unsent Letter From the Muse*
>*Overture*
>*Seduction*
>*Jesse 3*

Jennifer O'Shea   80

>*Friend*
>*An Idyllic Dream of the Soul Mates*
>*Harvest Moon*
>*Before I Was a Mother*
>*Back from War*

Pat Severin   90

>*The Call I Heed*
>*A Love Like Ours*
>*Our Love's Not Complicated*
>*A Love Letter to Women Who Love Shoes*
>*Our Love Story*

Denis Murphy   100

>*Who Cares for the Carer?*
>*Troubled Times*
>*Fly Away My Butterfly*
>*Chasing Memories*
>*Another Fool*

Alshaad Kara   108

>*Nickname*
>*Rules of Love*
>*The Duet of Angels*
>*The Encomium*

Cynthia Bernard   114

>*Love Songs*
>*Once Upon a Time*
>*Moving In*
>*Leaving*

John Wiley   122

>*Girl in the Full Metal Jacket*
>*Flirt*
>*Love is Best*
>*I Wish*

Jerri Hardesty   128

>*Sensing*
>*Three Woods*
>*Creative Living*
>*Lovesong*

Thomas Zampino   136

Just One Word
Through Thirty-Five Years
You Have Always Known That

Lynn White   140

Bury Me Deep
Don't Go
Dreaming

Tasneem Hossain   144

Endless Love
Spring Sojourn
Be My Love

Joan McNerney   150

I See You in Bright Colors
Noontime
Wildflowers

Rhian Elizabeth   154

cease fire
death of a sunflower
it starts like this

Richard M. Bañez   158

A Villanelle for Love and Marriage
Dear Self
Hide and Seek

Mark Fleisher   164

Come to My Dreams
The Best Time
Into the Essence

April Garcia   168

Kisses from a Bottle
So Much More
Unholy Love

Ram Krishna Singh (R K Singh)   172

Fount of Poetry

Doug Croft   174

Your Beautiful Heart
I Love You

S Afrose   177

My Love

Matt J. McGee   180

It Happen the Night You Sneezed

Connie Carmichael   182

The Kiss

C. A. MacKenzie   184

Flowers of Love
To My Future Valentine

Jackie Chou   188

> *Formosa*
> *Love Poem*

Emily Bilman   192

> *Love's Reply*
> *Initiation*

Dvora Robinson   196

> *Your Skin as Warm as a Rock*

Shirsak Ghosh   199

> *Close Encounters*

Adrian Ernesto Cepeda   203

> *Real Intimacy*

Cai Quirk   206

> *Iridescent Silver*

Erica Ellis   211

> *Entire Nation*
> *Galileo*

Allan Lake   220

> *No Secret Anymore*

Laurice E. Tolentino   222

> *Paternal Love*
> *Independency*

Sara L. Uckelman   226

    Nequeo, Nequis, Nequit

Douglas M. Lynn   228

    Angel of Love

LindaAnn LoSchiavo   230

    Valentine Villanelle
    Twilight in Italy with Phoenix

Meaghan M. Murphy   234

    Desperately and Silently, I Love You
    Today I Bring for You

Sakariyahu A. Jamiu   238

    Letter to the Treasure

Donna Kathryn Kelly   240

    Dusk Love Sonnet
    The Day Before the Day Before Valentine's Day in
      Year Two of the Pandemic

Gitanjli Mridul   243

    Soul Baring

Mary Ann Cabuyao Abril   246

    On the Day We Meet

Glenda M. Dimaano   249

    I'll Look After You

Sophie Jupillat Posey   252

> *Traveler*
> *Lightning*

Amanda Valerie Judd   258

> *Doug*

Christine M. Du Bois   260

> *French Toast*

Ken Gosse   262

> *Sweet Pen of Youth*
> *Advice from a Father to His Daughter and her Beau*

Bill Cushing   269

> *Morning*
> *A Suadela's Shardoma*

Liwanag C. Rubico   273

> *The End of Exodus*

Teejay D. Panganiban   275

> *Leap of Faith*
> *Treasured Love: A Tapestry of Joy and Pain*

Michael H. San Miguel   280

> *Forever My Anchor*

Moe Phillips   282

    Lovers on the Brink

Marianne Tefft   285

    You Have Never Seen the Ocean

Jone MacCulloch   288

    Night Mysteries

Carol Edwards   290

    Blinded
    Love, Observed

Previous 2022 anthologies
    from Southern Arizona Press   294

Upcoming 2023 anthologies
    from Southern Arizona Press   296

New independent releases
    From Southern Arizona Press   298

Published works by our featured contributors   302

Linda M. Crate is a Pennsylvanian writer whose poetry, short stories, articles, and reviews have been published in a myriad of magazines both online and in print. She has twelve published chapbooks: *A Mermaid Crashing Into Dawn* (Fowlpox Press - June 2013), *Less Than A Man* (The Camel Saloon - January 2014), *If Tomorrow Never Comes* (Scars Publications, August 2016), *My Wings Were Made to Fly* (Flutter Press, September 2017), *splintered with terror* (Scars Publications, January 2018), *More Than Bone Music* (Clare Songbirds Publishing House, March 2019), *the samurai* (Yellow Arrowing Publishing, October 2020), *Follow the Black Raven* (Alien Buddha Publishing, July 2021), *Unleashing the Archers* (Guerilla Genesis Press, August 2021), *Hecate's Child* (Alien Buddha Publishing, November 2021) *fat & pretty* (Dancing Girl Press, June 2022), and *Searching Stained Glass Windows For An Answer* (Alien Buddha Publishing, December 2022). She is also the author of the novella *Mates* (Alien Buddha Publishing, March 2022).

wildflowers

when she holds my hand,
calls my name,
speaks her truths,
whispers her stories,
and sings our songs i feel
my heart melt into a thousand
shades of rainbows;
each shade sending birds into the
universe with different names until
even sunsets know our clouds—

we hold each other through
sorrow, through joy, through anger
and bitter disappointments;

we share our hurts and our pains and our scars—

then we build our dreams and make them
realities,
blooming like wildflowers;

no amount of concrete could ever stop our love
from growing.

this is our kingdom

we stand together
in the forest, in fields
of wildflowers,
in the sea, in the mountains,
through troubles and joys;

we wear the jewels of one
another's happy tears and sad tears as crowns—

together we know home isn't a place but
rather a person,
and she is my sun and i am her moon;

i often imagine a world where we can be together
and no one bats an eye at the fact we're wives—

because life is difficult enough
with all of it's bitterness and nightmares without
having to worry about other people trying to
crash through all the panels of your love,

shattering the stained glass to cut you and the one
you adore;

but i will be her knight and drive away every
dragon and ill hearted prince and king
that tramp into our kingdom thinking they have
any authority; because this our kingdom and i will not
let them destroy our trees or flowers.

shine and bloom

when you kiss me,
i feel the light of a thousand
stars singing in my veins;
and every dead flower in me
blooms once more because
they've realized
we're home—
some people think home is a place,
but it's really in the hearts of all
those who house us;
and you house the most of me
every piece i was too afraid or embarrassed
to share with everyone else—
you know my dreams and my secrets,
and i know yours;
through thick and thin we're building
a world where we both can
shine and bloom;
a world where our darkness and light can
both be celebrated because both are
required to make a day.

true love never dies

you wear dawn and white roses
in a crown,
that lights up everything
around you;

when evening comes you exchange
it with a crown of sunsets and lilies—

but always you are blooming,
until i let you know that it is okay to rest;
and you let me wear my crown
of moons and sunflowers—

together we dance in light and darkness,
obliterating all obstacles in our path;

making our dreams reality—

our hearts are twined time after time
in this world and the next and the one after
because true love never dies.

this love of mine

i was caught in a thick winter's ice
before you thawed me out,
reminding me that the dreaming wasn't
dead when i was still alive;

you were the fae that brought back
the seasons when i thought i would forever
be trapped in the talons of a cruel winter—

you reminded me that i was beautiful
scars and all, taught me that i wasn't as alone as
i thought i was and showed me that there
were flowers and butterflies left in this world
that i had not met;

you introduced me to new stars and new moons—

a new season bloomed in me after you
restored everything in me that i thought was
dead and gone forever,

and in exchange this love of mine will forever be yours.

you are the sun and i am your moon

hold my hand,
the rest of the world
can fade;

you restore me in
a smile—

your kiss, the softness
of your hands, your
lips pressed against mine
in the sweet honey of their
whispers;

you house my dreams and i house yours—

together we conquer every problem,
so when i am with you i am not afraid;
i know with you i walk in secure footing
wherever we go—

your laughter is the song that heals
all the ills in my world,

you are the sun and i am your moon.

Michael Thomas Ellis is an author, long in the tooth and sporadic in inspiration, but has been published in *The Talking Stick, Open Arts Forum, Sunlight Press, Waymark, Tuck Magazine, Dark Sire,* the anthology *Moving Images: Poetry Inspired by Film, Anti-Heroin Chic, Cajun Mutt, Loud Coffee Press, Riddled With Arrows, EveryWriter,* and frequently in his favorite daily breakfast treat, *The Drabble.*

Purr

I am not a gnarled desire grasping
for a younger persuasion
nor a groomed garden cutting
to be tossed once withered.

I may have veined hands
and sweetbreads not fresh-baked
but I laugh deliciously
and live to knead your dreams.

So let me be your Persian cat
dug deep in the quilts
to be remembered
and found
without thinking

and I will reward you

with my purr.

A Short Tribute to the Word Quiver

She called it *a perfect afternoon*
we had just left a poetry reading
and were enjoying our coffees
on a café couch beneath a red umbrella
slightly shaded from the hot Florida sun.

We were reading some of the short ones
from a thick book of Octavio Paz poems
that she had just purchased
to compensate the bookstore owner
for hosting such a fine event.

Very quickly it became apparent
that dear Octavio had a thing for
the word *quiver* which he used
multiple times across a few of the
early poems at the front of the book.

She said she really liked that word
which of course set me all aquiver
so I had no choice but to write her
this poem that I knew she would like
because it uses a word she likes.

And because she also confessed
she liked the short ones the best
I will resist getting too carried away
unless I have done so already
and I will end it right here right now.

A Thousand Pebbles

I crabbed along the shore today
gathered up a thousand pebbles
maybe fewer
maybe more
and carried them to the clifftop
in search of flaws
with gentle eyes and probing fingers
yes
but searching nonetheless
in hopes of finding one
just one
that promised something more
just one
that I might keep
while tossing back the others
one by one
some with care
some nonchalant
some hard in anger
but almost always
with a certain disappointment
down to the shore below.

There were smooth ones
rough ones
small ones
round ones
and flat ones by the score
quite a few were ivory
others milky brown
some were even gold
some were just
cheap chunks of sparkling glass
that cut me just to hold
yet all had some allure

but it was odd
how almost every one of them
left me wanting more
some
just a little more
for those few
I would hesitate
give a second look
then sigh
cock my wrist
and send them back home
to that crowded ocean floor.

I spent a lot of time today
sifting through those gems
until only one remained
an exquisite little heart of stone
as if freed from my own ribs
then shrunk
to make it easier to hold
tan and slight
with a vein of white
running east to west
I marveled at its simplicity
its innocence
for it was not
gaudy
shiny
sparkling
gleaming
nor laced with veins of precious gold
still
it caught my eye
and I couldn't let go
besides
it felt so remarkably right
just resting there
cupped
in the palm of my hand
I couldn't let go.

So I stood up slowly
back aching a bit
legs shaking from the squatting
and the years
and lifted up that heart of stone
to the glancing fading light
and smiled
tossed it up and caught it
gently
and laughed
this is it
this is the one
    the one I would keep
and of course
it was the last
of those thousand pebbles.

Yes
you I would keep
if you will have me
but please
do not examine me in turn
too closely
or you will see
I am just another pebble
with imperfections of my own.

Soft Parade of Sighs

I asked her to propose to me
ten times that she be sure
should the wind escort my wings
to light upon her door?

Her troubled conscience paramount
beleaguered by her heart
she tried her love to exorcise
though it swamped her every thought.

But in private revelations
she has seen beyond the course
of rivers twisted from their banks
by fears without remorse.

She has she has come back to love!
in her voice it writhes
like I she cannot do without
this soft parade of sighs.

Leonid

Say my name
shout it to the stars
so all shall hear
and exclaim at the magnificence
in your voice
now
while the stars fall from the sky
on this night of heaven to earth
say you love me
a hundred times
no
a thousand times
over
and I will echo your words
and your love
into the depths
of the night.

Sunrise Sunset

At sunrise
I saw her picture
read her words
and sensed a love recalled
a memory gathered
from some time
before our own.

Balancing
against that frail wind
seized
by those impossible mornings
so slow to believe
the arrogance in me
finally wilted
and gave in to love.

I looked up
as she came to me
moonlit
piercing love's surface
pushing apart
its slick black waters
under that star-crossed
California sky
and I followed her
no matter where
it might lead
to what we both
were sure
was waiting.

For she was apricots
with scents delicious
beyond molten myrrh
a lovely luring bazaar
before which I had to linger
and longed to taste.

At her table
of ripe tomatoes
and orange-scented rhymes
my tongue came alive
and so I ate
heartily
and loved her
with my words.

Perfectly lovely
were her clavicles
delicious and soft
her generous tears
and so open and willing
was she
for what she thought
she saw
in me.

So utterly gorgeous
was this new and playful love
flirting foolishly
awash in serendipities
such a tender laughing devotion
a hunger as yet
too joyful to imagine
any alternatives.

Laugh for me!
I would say
her eyes flashing in reprise
open wide
those soft dusky windows
and reveal without fear
the flawed interiors
I can no longer breathe
without.

For I inhaled her life
And she my own.

Then wide-eyed came
the carnal dreamscape
that palette
of promising morsels
made for mouths
ravenous with ecstasy
the sweet taste
of sweeter pleasures
from the sweetest
of bodies erupted.

Afternoons
I would find her
radiant in heat
stretched out
long and white-legged
uplifted
inviting me
to please dance
with her
awhile.

Come swollen
her eyes would say
split my body gladly
that my eager invitation
be pleased
by your choosing.

And so
the musk would spill
on hands
stroked by bodies
richly salted
delicious with sweat
yes dancing
to that ancient rhythmic beat
of noise and desire.

Until finally
our love could rest
and I in the stillness of shadows
would rearrange
her moonstruck hair
and endure the long fall
of darkness
to light.

For nothing
quenched my craving
as the sight of my love
at sunrise
freed to be by me
lingering
with no swinging bridges
or taunting cliffs
to dangle the joy
above.

And so
for a time
our love roamed free
untethered
drifting gently within
the calm
but there were gargoyles
always gargoyles
looking down
laughing
waiting.

So it was
on that winter morning
cold and hemmed in
by a soul-numbing snow
my scarf failed her
and she began to shiver
for the comforts
of a safer
and more certain
climate.

Love's Mount trembled
Love itself cracked open
The Passion was swallowed
And the Dying began.

Oh yes doubt does its work
roughly but surely
with practiced hands
sculpting a rutting guilt
with stone-crushing enthusiasm
until love cannot help
but be demolished.

Say farewell
to the succulent indulgence!
once so ripe with believing
pity the poor naïve fool
who hopes to savor
such a splendid setting
such a tangled feast
for the miserly term
of a whole life.

The wildest of sorrows
had swallowed us
while those three Ghosts
stood by idly
barely whispering
entreating us
to hold fast
to a vibrant wonder.

Why won't they intervene
speak up!
or give us some kind of sign
a clear one to light up
this fading path of dreams
and if so
would we even read it rightly
or would we simply
turn our heads away
in fear and disbelief?

Doubt bellowed!
and made the choice for us
buffeting us
bullying us
ripping away
this waltz of pleasure
and in so doing
damned
our self-denying hearts.

It seems
no love
is safe
when it longs
for too much
it breaks
and heaven
turns its eyes
elsewhere.

Disappointment
pounded breathless
in my chest
on that cold winter's morn
when I sighed
donned my armor
and went to face my enemy
my fear
my stricken
love.

Drowning
in farewells
we parted
while off in the distance
abandoned
our souls shrieked
objecting in unison
to the foolishness
of such a love
forsaken.

Now dusk
comes down hard
meaningless shadows
float madly
across bare dusty floors
hissing
with regrets
over crumbling bits
of forgotten
prayers.

I sit here
broken
still wrestling
a joyless desire
crying out
damn love!
while still grasping at it
thinly
with unsteady
sweaty
empty hands.

I know I know
the kisses
have been packed
but they will always
be remembered
every nightfall
like now
when sorrow's grip
once again
tears the dark
from yet one more
bleeding
sunset.

 **James Thomas Fletcher** is native to Oklahoma but has steamed down the Amazon and up the Nile, hiked the Sonoran Desert, climbed the Great Pyramid, sailed the Atlantic, skydived Oklahoma, scuba dived the Pacific, and snowshoed in Canada. He has lived in a tenth-century Cistercian Monastery in Belgium, the Piedmont of the Carolinas, a protected heron rookery beside the Great Lakes, the Acadian bayous of Louisiana, the shortgrass prairie of the Great Plains, and on the side of a volcano in the rain and cloud forests of the Republic of Panamá.

Academically, he holds a Master of Arts in English degree in Creative Writing–Poetry and has eighteen poetry collections in print.

He has picked cotton, made fiberglass and, in hazmat suit, cleaned filters inside a nuclear laundry. He was a combat infantryman in Vietnam, company clerk at North Atlantic Treaty Organization Supreme Headquarters Allied Powers Europe, (NATO/SHAPE), bartender in South Carolina, bricklayer in Oklahoma, oil field chainhand in Louisiana, roustabout in the Gulf of Mexico, English instructor in North Carolina, and Director of Computer-Aided Instruction at the University of Illinois in Chicago.

For more information visit:
https://linktr.ee/jamesthomasfletcher

Love Letters in Poetic Verse

Postcard from Now

Light bends around the sun
or any gravitational mass.
You once wrote that you found
yourself bending to my words.

I thought of the physics first
but your meaning was Matrixical.
Still I liked the thought and, as I bend
to yours as well, this is apropos:

As twin suns we bend,
like light past gravity,
to one another's words.
Meaning drawn as tides to the moon.

Apparition

Dear Betty,

Once I wrote, "Have you thought I'd forgotten you?"
Your letter arrived, your birthday passed.
I rise, work, eat, sleep. And study. And study
the past, your part in the past, your absence
from my future. The gaps in the present that belong
to you. Our flame convulses and explodes, never warms.

You remain aloof, aloft, alone, above my little pain.
Once we were distracted by lifestyles and commitments
that I refused to fully accept. Do you love me
for my frankness? or curse my lingering?

The price of many items is abstention from others.
My beautiful abstention, this letter is an assurance
that, funneled through however many sources, diluted
through distance of years and miles, however mollified,
modified, and disguised, I offer my love.

I saw you last in white, in a Japanese garden
in a city destroyed. Your smile intact.
Intact. Whole. Complete. Flawless.
    You died without a hint.
This email address is no longer valid.
Your death announced itself without emotion.

Return through stellar dust, through sub-atomic
particle fields, through radio waves in plasma,
through the ghostly visage of Houdini.
Return — Return your Death to Sender
if only in my dreams.

Jim

Quantum Entanglement

Sometimes it seems that you sit
half a country and a quarter
of a century away
and taunt me to cross again these bounds.

I know this is me feeling frustrated
because I want to offer you
one of my lives, one that is all yours.
But I only have one.
And I do not know how to give you
a piece of a life.

Wistful yearnings fit our designated karma
yet marriage would be disaster.
In a parallel universe, like two suns
colliding, we would have ruptured.
But gravity and physics, or kismet and desire,
may have caused us to live a life apart
only to remarry later with an immutable bond.

Or maybe the sky is always bluer
on the other side of the universe.

These scenarios unfold within
my mind's playful eye.
Ripen amid whimsy. Still
you are meant
to be someone haunting and cosmic
in my life, or my previous life,
or my next lives, or something.

Through all the miles and time
we are connected
on many levels. We emit radiation
like gravity that tugs at us no matter
how far we distance ourselves.

Maybe I am not supposed to figure us out.
But your gravity always controls my tides.

Star-Quaker

Dear Ms. Harper,

You misunderstood my message. How could we
have a conversation that wasn't built upon cryptic
comments, Iseric gaps, and intra-line interpretation?
But there you be. Upon my page again,
with your pixie dust and pirouettes, double entendres
oozing from each swollen-tipped word like a flower
forcing its nectar at the gods, yet willing
to allow a humble bee its stinging nirvana.

You say, "I can only lose." Ah the first typo.
I typed, "I can only love." But you speak
in riddles when you throw my own lines back to me.
In these chronicles, you offer many answers.
I offer lazy responses, the languid prose of inner
voice and drawn-out thoughts.

I should unlock myself from this text
and freefall, but I feel the tug of direction
pulling me to words even as the words
diverge, becoming wayward thoughts. A flippancy,
sometimes expressed, sometimes edited.

People no longer speak to one another.
Perhaps that's why we ended at the computer
again. A breaking of ice. The intimacy
of computer providing new context.
You ask probing questions with a unique
sense of analysis. I gain much but not much
to carry away.

Love Letters in Poetic Verse

Write of the lake and you but not too much,
for I cannot return in favor but I will reply
in snatches. Whirl me once again about your wee hours,
the ghost in the computer, and without frightening
the kitten on your lap, dust off my image and do
with it as you please (within cybernetic reason).

Love and Kisses, Jim

Spelunking the Past

Do you remember touring Fantastic Caverns
on our frantic trip thirty-three years ago?
We rode a tram through the cave.
Inside they took a group photo.

I had forgotten that side junket
of our wild cross-country excursion
until I found this picture minutes ago.

It is black and white but you
are wearing my green jacket and beret.
I am in shirtsleeves wearing my heart there.

The photo is hazy and blemished
but we are there, joined
and bound in time, carved in stone,
as it were, for one moment in eternity.

I loved you.
How can you be dead?

The Third Solar Cycle

My favorite New Year's was not long ago
on a private dock in the Pee Dee River
behind a house off Pawley's Island.
Meteors sprinkled the crisp sky and the party
noises were distinct but vague. Splashing
and moonlight were more pronounced.

The New Year approaches.
Our third. And according to tradition
we get one physical meeting for each solar cycle.
Coffee on Michigan Avenue?
Chamber music in Palatine, academic meeting
on campus, educational conference, computer expo,
such limiting choices. But possibilities
nonetheless. Whether tea or rusty nails
(or biting nails or scratching walls)
the future quaintly holds the answer.

I relish time to talk with you, squeezing it
in now as the hurricane swirls to pass me and I
imagine my calendars and clocks sucked
through its whirlpool leaving me spinning
in the wake. Thus I linger.

So I lingered on her thighs a fateful moment.

But your thighs are as abstract
as Cohen's quisling rendezvous above.
Your trenchant words the allure of our bond.
Once the rooster of the New Year has crowed
will I find you on my doorstep once again?

**Swayam Prashant** (pen-name of Dr. Prashanta Kumar Sahoo) was born in the undivided Cuttack district, Odisha. He was formerly an Associate Professor of English at Sarupathar College, Assam, India. He has written six books and two booklets: *Evaluation of Textbooks in the Teaching of English* (based on his Ph.D. thesis); *Values in Life* (based on a research project on Vedic and Upanishadic writings); *Knowledge Tree* (miscellaneous prose writings); *Haiku from the Garden of My Own* (poetry); *Live Like a Man* (poetry); *Premras Amrit* (poetry in Assamese); *Virgin Land Impregnated* (a thematic study of Canadian folk songs); and *Joy of Love* (a unique booklet of love poems).

Love Letters in Poetic Verse

Will You Be My Valentine?

If you don't see anything in me to love
you are blind
You only see my flesh and skin
Why don't you see that I love
what YOU love
Why don't you see that I tread the path
that you tread
Why don't you see that I sing the song
that you sing ?
I love every curve
of the calligraphy of your life's handwriting
Every inch of you is me.
Don't you love yourself ?
If you love yourself
you love me
You and me are not different
we are one.
I love you and you love me.
And O how sweet sweet it will be
if you become my valentine !

An Open-eyed Dream

You are a dream I see
with my eyes open.
Your beauty inspires me
to give wings to my words
and flames to my ideas,
O my Muse !
(hail Imagination !)
But do you inspire me
or my idea of you does ?
Do I love you
or my own reflection in you*?
Still you are required as a medium
for creation.
Words are crafted and moulded
into timeless shapes, O my Muse,
with your inspiration.

Footnote :
* Echo of Rumi's idea of 'reflection of beauty'

Thirst Alive

Come, Trishna
I have been waiting for you so long;
give your hand,
let us walk
in the lanes and by-lanes
among the rows of green trees,
blooming flowers,colourful butterflies
and humming honey bees.

In spite of struggles and wars, quarrels and
                                                            fights,
sorrows and sufferings, and tensions and
                                            unhappiness
that the life is fraught with everyday
once again we are under the rainbow-bathed
                                            sky.

After you left me ages ago
I forgot to notice   such beauties...
Now that you have come back to me
poetry seems to be alive everywhere.
With your return
words have got back their voice
and Nature has become vibrant again.

Arch Beauty

I had never thought you to be charming
until I noticed the arch of your eyebrows
I decided to celebrate its beauty
with the brush of a painter
I had never thought you to be sweet-speaking
until I heard the music of your voice
I tried to preserve its rhythm
in the beats of my heart
I had never thought you to be graceful
until I observed the gaiety of your footsteps
I wished to recreate the movements
by capturing them in a dance
but I did not succeed in any
until you loved me, dear Honey.

A Century of Love

Ten poems are yet to be written
to complete an honourable century;
my pen has become dry of ink
my brush has become dry of colours –
only if you touch me
with your red soft lips
soaking me in the sweet
colours of love
the pen will again be filled with words
the brush will again be wet with colours
the songs will be sung with a golden symphony
to complete one hundred.

Eduard Schmidt-Zorner is a translator and writer of poetry, haibun, haiku, and short stories.

He writes in four languages: English, French, Spanish, and German and holds workshops on Japanese and Chinese style poetry and prose and experimental poetry.

He is a member of four writer groups in Ireland. He has lived in County Kerry, Ireland, for more than 30 years and is a proud Irish citizen, born in Germany.

He has been published in over 190 anthologies, literary journals, and broadsheets in United States of America, United Kingdom, Ireland, Australia, Canada, Japan, Sweden, Spain, Italy, Austria, France, Bangladesh, India, Mauritius, Nepal, Pakistan, and Nigeria.

Some of his poems and haibun have been published in the French (own translation), Romanian, and Russian languages.

He also writes under his penname Eadbhard McGowan.

Found You

I found you as a counterpart,
and hold your hand.
Smells and taste of vanilla, herbs,
I discover oases and hills,
valleys with all their secrets.

I play with you on mystic strings,
unlock unknown sounds
which ether away,
fade like the melodic clink
of piano tunes
conjured by ivories.

Your breath in my ear,
words whispered into your hair,
we sink into love,
and drown
in a warm embrace.
Your lips entice me
to kiss ripe fruits
from cherry branches.

Attar, made
from the essence,
of roses, herbs, and spices.
A drop on your lips
a drop on my skin.
You are like the wine
from the *Languedoc*
a taste on the tongue,
overwhelming, floral, ripe,
with a taste of the autumn sun.

For Baroness M.

It seems to me
that I met You once,
thousand years ago.

I think it was
between *Euphrates* and *Tigris*
or as stardust in space,
flying past each other.

Or long before the time in the taiga.

Souls, not yet sedentary,
hovered over the Baltic Sea,
destined
to meet again one day,
to talk about mysterious premonitions
which inherent experiences
obscurely whisper to us.

I see the familiar now differently,
feel strange thoughts,
follow ideas and traces.

Maybe I will find
a way to you again,
that I never dreamed of?

Your Hand in Mine

Wind from the north-west
grooms the coat of wild horses,
We observe the starry sky,
contemplate moon's shine,
enjoy the choir of crickets
singing into the night.
Holding me to prevent a fall;
your hand rests in mine.

Croatian Memories

I saw at the market stand
on *Svetog Marka* Place
your serious face.
I asked for the reason,
of your sadness,
which remained unanswered,
but you told me
the reason
before dawn.

We went through *Zagreb*,
hand in hand,
made stops at taverns,
sang heartbreaking songs,
we sang *Ima dana,
kada ne znam šta da radim.**
We sang against the establishment.

We drank plum brandy,
wine of the Adriatic,
read poems together
of Croatian writers
until late into the night,
we followed the lines
searched for hidden signs.

I lost sight of you.
The regret is still there,
not passed after decades,
a desire for restitution,
has remained,
also the hopelessness
of days gone by, irrevocably,
to make up for the missed opportunity,
to catch up again.

Tried for years to find you.
You have left no traces,
at least I could not discover any,
the shroud of finality
is spread over it.

In *Zagreb*, there is, ironically,
a *'Museum of Broken Relationships'*
from romances that withered
to broken connections,
mementoes left over
after a relationship ends.

*("There are days
when I don't know what to do,
because this song causes me pain,
I love you so deeply that I could die,
I love you, but I don't know why".)

Notes of Times Gone By

I met you in *Gorky Park*
on a Sunday afternoon,
a day with minus 10 degrees,
it became dark, soon
icy winds from the taiga blew,
trees were covered
in heavy snow.

It flew over a spark,
and lit my heart.
We met every day
in the park
we shared the same way,
went hand in hand
in full harmony
hoped that there
would be no end.

Sat in the venerable library
of the *Lomonosov* University,
and stuck our heads,
cheek to cheek,
into many books
and read *Lermontov*,
empathised with writers,
felt the desperation
of *Fyodor Dostoevsky*,
and saw our reflection
in the verses of *Pushkin*.

Love Letters in Poetic Verse

Gorky Park

Jamie Santomasso is a poet from Kansas City, Missouri. A writer since the age of five, she has used the literary arts as a means to express her thoughts and feelings through the written word.

Jamie takes inspiration from both life experience and imagination to create vivid pictures of love, heartbreak, fantasy, darkness, and other residual thoughts. Her works have received praise for their ability to evoke emotion, paint, pictures, and tell stories that the reader can fully immerse and lose themselves in.

Jamie has been published in several online and print productions, including anthology works from *Impspired*, the *Rio Grande International Poetry Festival*, and *300 South Media Group*.

Ode to the Fire

When the words she speaks steals your breath
and your pounding heart skips a beat
and your stone walls come crashing down
just remember my love to breathe

She's the wind that guides your sails
when your war ship is lost at sea
raise your white flag and surrender
she's the one that will set you free

Because your heart has found its home
on the path that you were once lost
she'll take your hand and lead you back
through the barren lands you had crossed

Rest your weary soul in her arms
she'll heal the wounds that your heart bares
her words will nurse you back to health
mend the scars that your body wears

When you finally know that's she's the one
that speaks forever in your name
your fire meant to blaze together
two souls that burn from the same flame

Galaxy's Billet-doux

I'm a supernova, dying radiant light
I'm lost in the explosion's pull
She saves me from my celestial fate
She pulls me from my black hole

She is the earth, her grace the atmosphere
And her love is the gravity
She pulls me into to her magnetic orbit
I'm falling with terminal velocity

I am the moon, Earth's lunar kiss
Humble servant to her, the sun
Unshielded from her fiery fury
She bleeds passion that can't be undone

She is the heavens, Elysian Skies
My paradise come fruition
Her open gates call me home
I have the ticket, but she grants admission

I am the fire, burning high
She is the air breathing life into me
May she always blow her winds my way
And set my raging blazes free

i'll carry your heart

i will carry the weight of your heart, and

carry the pain it's felt. I will carry

your burden of heartache, and the trials it's been dealt. I will carry your

heart [when you're not strong enough to carry it on your own]

with my hands I will carry it [so that you're not alone]. You may call

me when your tears may fall, and

i will be your rock. I'll

carry your heart [with me] , alone

it will never walk. I'll carry your heart

[*in* my chest] so we will never be apart,

my love knows no bounds, so I'll always carry your

heart

Tribute to e.e. cumming's "[i carry your heart with me(i carry it in]

Wilted Rose

Some roses may wilt in summer's sun, and
say the heat was a force too strong.
The strongest buds and petals in the
world can only hold strength for so long.
Will you turn cheek and let my red rose die; in the
end, life and bloom return tenfold;
in knowing my rose will live on past death, the
fire of the sun will never have its hold.
Some roses may wilt in winter's cold, and
say that the blizzard was too long,
in knowing that love can never be frozen
ice will never take away its sweet song.
From death is born life and my love is
what lives, I will always be devoted to you
I've felt your soft petals between my fingers, and
tasted the sweet nectar of you too.
Of roses that wilt I will never take for granted, my
desire will lift a dying bud to bloom.
I hold your rose close, next to my heart and
hold my desire within until my tomb.
With my last request I'll water your stem
those who deny your thirst be damned
who leave you in the sun to burn, only do so in
favor of earning judgement and remand.

...*Fire* of the sun will never have its hold.

Tribute to Robert Frost's "Fire and Ice"

She

And when she looks at me,
all the despair and all
that's heavy in my heart lifts. The
best of her spirit and the light
of her soul breathes into me. The
dark that paints my skies shifts to sun,
and the clouds that pour give way to the
bright. And if our fingertips were to
meet once more, and our lips touch
in silence, I would give the world in
her name. For she is perfection in every
aspect of the word. Her breath whispers mercy,
and her gaze forgiveness. Time stands still
her presence, and love lives eternally in her
eyes

Tribute to "She Walks in Beauty" by Lord Byron

Love Letters in Poetic Verse

Lord Byron and Marianna Segati

Rp Verlaine lives in New York City. He has a Master of Fine Arts in creative writing from City College. He taught in New York Public schools for many years. His first volume of poetry, *Damaged by Dames & Drinking*, was published in 2017 and another, *Femme Fatales Movie Starlets & Rockers*, in 2018. A set of three e-books titled *Lies From The Autobiography* vol 1-3 were published from 2018 to 2020. His newest book, *Imagined Indecencies*, was published in February of 2022. He was nominated for a Pushcart prize in poetry in 2021 and 2022.

He has a Facebook page with 0ver 32,000 followers at:

https://www.facebook.com/people/Rp-Verlaine/100066822182013/

Beginnings

Do not ask me of others, let's start fresh.
As if we were rare seedlings in the spring
sprouting promises with our sweetest thoughts
rooted deep beyond earthly wants of flesh.
Beyond true love's lost dark imaginings
pale jealousies , tides of mistrust wrought.
Let ardor beckon, wondrously new
we'll be its play things-puppets in a dance.
Outside the present to postpone regret
by giving love each day its place, while true
to ourselves, mocking fate's uneven chance
diving to we know not - to come out blessed.
So let's begin, without a sin or stain
after I ask you this-what is your name?

Unsent Letter From the Muse

My dear friend, I guess the question is this:
you live to dream in worlds of pretty words
of fanciful thoughts and the darkest truths
with words that arouse me to truly wish
that they be true, even if truth is blurred,
in art or dreams or fantasies of youth.
I wish to be that beauty you speak of-
angelic yet demure, which I am not.
The mirror shows me less than your eyes see
speaking with reverence that's close to love:
your poems , sweet yet filled with tender shocks
capture my heart only to set it free.
My fear is soon, you'll see me as I am
and replace me, a thought I cannot stand.

Overture

If I write you a poem, should it rhyme
or be clever with words, so seldom used
a dictionary must be close to help?
If I write you a poem, with what design?
Will it be so profound as to confuse?
Would you prefer that I do something else?
Music's not my style and neither is dance
without touching once or moving as one.
Were I a jazz soloist, I'd bend notes
to shake the heavens, if given a chance.
But no, it seems that poetry's won
and this sonnet will do or so I hope.
But wait, sweet darling, I've run out of lines
I must start again-I hope you don't mind.

Seduction

the details of your body are matchless words
of a rare beauty that when brought together
form a defining enchantment that serves
to awe, to daze-to fantasize with forever
knowing that such dimension, such grace
were it a letter, could never detail enough
were it a mirror, you'd see my brave face
dropping all its pretense, to stare at love
be it illusory but surely no less true
than the smoke from a satyr's caress
be it star crossed but of stars still hued
burning like lamps to blot out my emptiness
truly my love-your body, touch and grace
I will want forever, or at least- till daybreak.

Jesse 3

Jess, we're trifles , dust from the distant stars
some argue specks traveled from far beyond
perhaps we're issue that Adam's rib carved
or the faint echo from cave men long gone...
The marks we leave often faint then erased
from sculptured stone to cinemas black fade
from my songs to you, to singers who chase
fame in platinum or gold, mining their trade.
Most are forgotten, lost to empty time
a poet can only laugh with half tears
at being remembered past their last rhyme
which you deserve with beauty so dear.
You've become all my thoughts are undone by
a singular truth-which now multiplies.

Jennifer O'Shea lives in beautiful Minnesota, a place of transforming beauty. Her writings reflect the observations and synergy between the concept of her eternal spirit and the experiences she accumulates with nature and art.

She and her husband are building a cabin in the woods where she finds unlimited inspiration! Jennifer is able to connect with her inner child as she interacts with and immensely enjoys the view of the world through the eyes of her three grandchildren. Her golden doodle, River is a constant companion offering his unconditional love. During the day she finds great rewards as she teaches elementary students reading skills as a Reading Interventionist.

One of the poets she is inspired by the most is Hafiz, a Persian mystic poet.

She has published pieces in three separate volumes with Southern Arizona Press. Jennifer also has poems featured in a book of poems from Open Skies Poetry.

Friend

Your face at my door, dear friend of mine
A vision of love and care
Not treasure, or jewels, or riches untold
Could ever be measured to you there.

An Idyllic Dream of the Soul Mates

Your everlasting love will not, cannot let me go, nor would I ever desire it to.

It has planted seeds and blossomed a bounty of magnificence of enduring beauty in my heart and soul. We are bound by an ethereal power to which there is no undoing. Let us celebrate love tonight as we, in this exquisite moment, hold the reins of creation!

For you beloved, I begin by hypnotizing the moon to come a little closer so I may see your face in the light of it.

Then you will crush a thousand grapes with the rocks from celestial shores to create an elixir that causes our rendezvous to deepen.

Next, we offer our request to the angels to perform with cellos and harps and saxophones, their notes stirring within us a desire to sway on the wind to their buttery sounds.

My darling is the maestro, the metronome setting the pulse of my heart.

The rhythm designs a telegram, a message sent to the firmament to cue the aurora borealis under whose magical other worldly display we dance.

The evening birds restrain their hoots and calls and the stars wait to fall as it is our pure love that stalls all of nature to pause and watch from the world's stage.

Together we'll reverently ask the meadow to lay out it's soft green grasses to create a velvety place for us to rest, wrapped we are so completely that we become one.

We shall encourage the waters to be calm as glass so we may see the reflection of us as we make wishes under the captivating light of Orion and Venus.

Let our night of dreams never cease, promises never waiver and our passion be the ingredients of fairytales.

As we embrace each other, mesmerized by the band of the Milky Way feeling ecstasy to the core of our eternal souls, we in turn gather up our lifetimes gone by in divine remembrance and realize we are soul mates playing our harmonic score.

Surely the creator of time and space proclaimed this sacred love to open its gates and swirl its ribbon of confirmation to adorn our hearts and sprinkle us with the dust of stars and their ancient knowing.

And as the sun seemed to hold back it's dawn just for us, our love song crooned its way to the heavenly scribes to be permanently etched in the fabric of love and added to the chronicles with the music of the spheres.

Harvest Moon

It was September, their 9th wedding anniversary. Their favorite song, Harvest Moon by Neil Young was playing as they danced on the parquet floor. The ocean waves roared in the background and as fate would have it, a full moon rose off the horizon.

Earlier on the boardwalk as they made their way towards the music, he stopped and plucked a hibiscus from a bush and slid it behind her right ear. The look of longing in their eyes almost caused them to turn back, but they had come to dance.

The man held her so gently yet with complete control. Her fitted cobalt dress was well suited for the dance they'd learned. His starched white shirt was unbuttoned, and the narrow suspenders kept the billowing fabric tame.

Onlookers stared, drinks halfway to their mouths. Other dancers slowed and gave more of the floor to the couple lost in their duet of bodies. The breezes off the water accompanied them, humans and nature dancing. The winds stirring their hair and the lower ruffles of her skirts. He guided them as they moved as one, their feet sure.

Music ending, their gaze continued into the silence until the patrons erupted with applause. This broke their reverie. As they became aware, their faces softened with gracious smiles and a bow to the appreciative crowd. Hand in hand, the moonlight guiding them home, the couple decided they would visit this dance again next year, on another harvest moon.

An Ekphrastic Poem for Bill Brauer's Harvest Moon

Before I Was a Mother

Before I was a mother
I was so young and so carefree
I ate what I wanted, stayed up late
My body, a reliable monotony.

The time drew near when we
Decided for a baby
And soon enough the work paid off
A mother? The idea so heady!

Hard to believe when I was told
A baby was growing inside me
So, I read the books, I bought the things
And I became baby savvy.

Everything that I now eat
Everything I breathe
I consider this being I have yet to meet
My sole responsibility.

This may be my defining moment
I mused with dreamy consideration
A person I am growing,
The seriousness laced with elation.

My body keeps on changing
I morph and crave and choose
The priorities and future thoughts
My goal my love, is you.

It doesn't matter to me
If a girl or boy you be
This love that's growing alongside you
Is the greatest mystery.

And now you're in my arms
The pain and strain are through
Looking in your dark blue eyes
There nothing I wouldn't do.

I have the title "mother" now
I understand the power
Your newly honored advocate
Nature bestowed on me in that hour.

I've turned into a mama bear
A champion, defender
A place of nourishment and comfort
Handling you with hands so tender.

What could be more important than
Protecting you with love so passionate
I no longer recognize myself
    I've become a warrior, your greatest fanatic.

Back From War

Oh my love you're back at last
I've missed you whilst away
Hold me close don't let me go
Let's embrace til light of day.

I wondered many lonely nights
If you'd come back to me
If you were hurt, if you were dead
Darling my heart belongs to thee.

Touch your lips to mine my love
So I know you are here right now
Take off your sword unbutton your coat
Let's recite our vows.

I can't say tis day or night
No time exists for us
Eternal love like ours a gift
All around a holy hush.

My heart dost overflow
No joy compares to this
To look into your eyes- your soul
This place where I know bliss.

The Lovers Return
Nathaniel Currier, c1852

**Pat Severin** is a retired Christian school teacher living in Appleton, Wisconsin, where she has been writing and sharing her poetry for many years. She has been an active member of the Society of Children's Book Writers and Illustrators for the past four years. Her Christian poems have been published in four Christian Magazines, the *Agape* Review, the *Clayjar Review*, *The Way Back 2 Ourselves*, and *Pure in Heart Stories*. In addition to her poetry, she has written a heartfelt memoir of her mother's life.

Pat is thrilled to be featured in this, her fifth Southern Arizona Press Anthology. She is also published in, *I Chose You, Perfectly Imperfect Rescue Dogs and their Humans* and *Chicken Soup for the Soul: Lessons Learned From My Dog* in which she served as a contributor. Both books are available on Amazon..

One of her most rewarding endeavors has been writing poems of encouragement for people going through difficult times and health struggles which she sends out weekly in her original cards.

The Call I Heed

My heart beats full with happiness,
The world must know it all.
For love has called and charmed me so,
And I must heed the call.
You ask just what has captured me?
Why do I feel like this?
Alas, it is was my heart's desire,
And, oh, my lover's kiss!
Oh, joy, 'tis he that fills my heart
With this euphoric feeling,
That grants me such contentment, now,
That has my spirit reeling!
Could this be what I've yearned for,
The freeing of my heart
That gives me this sensation?
It is but only part
Of that which poets write about,
Composers must possess
To write such love songs lyrical,
Words lovers do profess.
I can but say that now, at last,
That thing for which I've longed
Has captured me, a prisoner, I,
'Tis here where I belong!

A Love Like Ours

Can love still stand the test of time?
Can marriage really be
The union of two hearts in one,
For all eternity?

We see so many fall apart,
So many tossed aside,
And yet there are a few that grow,
That deepen, that abide.

The two of us are those who grow,
For us love never fails
Because we know that love takes work,
And just what that entails.

We'll never have to say the words,
"Do you love me, I wonder?"
For like it says, we're ever joined,
"No man can tear asunder!"

I am yours and you are mine,
That's why I have to say,
That I celebrate our love,
every single day!

That's why when love like ours is found,
It needs no celebration
Because when love's forever,
It has no destination.

Love Letters in Poetic Verse

Our love will always show the world
That marriage tried and true,
Can be the best, is ever blest,
Because it's me and you!

Our Love's Not Complicated

My Dearest Love,

I wish that I could shower you with flowers,
And give you pounds of chocolates that you could eat for hours.
But some will say that flowers are the thing for which girls yearn
And though you'd love the candy, dear, your health is my concern.

So, darling, I will give to you what you give me each day,
A heart that always loves and cares in every single way,
A friend that you can talk to, who'll listen to your thoughts,
Who'll offer a perspective and support you at all costs.

I'll be your friend and confidant, I'll give you what you need,
And even be available to sometimes intercede...
If that's the thing you want from me, I'll do it without question.
Agree with you I may not do, but I'll honor your suggestion.

But all in all, I love you, dear, with all my heart can give.
I'll be your wife, your friend for life, as long as we shall live.
And I don't need a holiday to tell you all these things.
Every day's the perfect time because of what it brings.

Now, I could say it brings to me, the things that all say love,
Like hearts and flowers, thoughts of spring, a token turtle dove.
But though such things have often been with love associated,
I'd rather say, I Love You, Dear, and that's not complicated!

A Love Letter to Women Who Love Shoes

Dear Women,

You're predictable, you all have this affliction.
Your love of shoes can't be denied, I'd say it's an addiction.
It starts when you are very young, perhaps, it's Mary Janes.
No matter, it's the shoe that's IN, that's why the boys complain…

Because they think it's silly, the big fuss you make about them.
They just don't understand at all. You cannot live without them!
But secretly the boys have an obsession that's athletic.
It's shoes their favorite stars endorse, you girls say, "It's pathetic!"

Regardless, girls and boys love shoes, though you get more publicity.
The love of shoes for some can be a full-blown eccentricity.
And I confess I even grew up having such a bent.
I had a strong desire for shoes and this is what it meant:

The shoes must be the current style, no matter how they hurt
And more than that, must match the purse, was something I'd assert.

I grew up with those pointy toes, the shoes the IN girls wore.
If casual or dress-up shoes, they left our poor feet sore.

But that was just the way it was, like you, I followed suit.
I didn't know the end result, what came of our pursuit.
And now that I am older I have feet that don't conform,
I still love shoes but my old feet are hardly uniform…

Or even the same size, instead of one shoe, I need two.
For one foot measures one size, for the other that won't do.
A whole size larger, buy a second pair? Now that's expensive!
And clerks don't want to see my feet. Oh, no. They're apprehensive.

We women, what we're left with are two feet that paid the price
For wearing shoes that really hurt…but, boy, those shoes looked nice.
I'm sure, like me, you'd like to find a way you could go back
And pick your shoes for fit instead of fashion, that's a fact!

I'll close now with a hope that you will find a comfy shoe,
A shoe that's doesn't hurt your feet, and I'll be...

Searching, too,

Your Sad Sole-Sister

Our Love Story

A match made in heaven, a twosome sublime,
A marriage of soul mates that's forged over time,
Through good times and bad, through bad weather and fair,
Each knowing the other will always be there.

Composers and poets write volumes of this,
And don't forget flowers, some moonlight, a kiss.
A romantic image, but is it the truth?
Or is it mere fiction, the daydreams of youth?

But is love and marriage a simple equation,
The joining of hearts with a common persuasion?
It's divine intervention crossing paths, making one,
That has to be nurtured, each day's battle won.

It's deep understanding, forgiveness and care,
Daily devotion and promises shared.
When love stands that test, stands firm and stands strong,
There's no greater gift, it's love's gorgeous song.

That is the secret of love that's forever,
A tie that is bound that no one can sever.
I know what that means and I know what that's worth,
For that's our love story, our treasure on earth.

True Love Dances

 **Denis Murphy** was born in 1959 in Cork, Ireland and now resides in Sligo, Ireland. He was a former Travel Consultant and Travel Agency Manager. A major turning point in his life came in 2007 when, at the age of 48, he was diagnosed with Parkinson's Disease. Anyone who suffers from this Disease, or has a family member who does, will know that it brings about drastic changes. It can be very difficult for people with Parkinson's to express their emotions, feelings and their loss of power and independence. All the more need for an outlet to express these emotions. He believes by sharing he can better understand what he is going through. One can get caught up in their own worries and forget that the disease not only affects their own lives, but also that of family, friends, and loved ones. They often feel as frustrated and confused as he does. He is very lucky to have such an understanding wife who has great patience, empathy, and understanding and provides her support, encouragement, inspiration, and love. The main themes of his poems are about coping with Parkinson's Disease, and his relationship with nature, life and with oneself. Poetry helps him appreciate this wonderful gift of life.

Who Cares for the Carer?

She spends her nights and days
Showing her love in so many ways
That gentle touch
That says so much
In selfless acts and unconditional love
An iron hand in a velvet glove
In a constant battle against the tide
Her worries and fears she tries to hide
The nights are long and often sleepless
Tossing and turning and very restless
Denied the comfort only sleep can bring
Ready for action, if his alarm should ring
Sometimes it is so hard to hold back the tears
When she thinks of the future with anxiety and fears
Some days she is too tired to feel
But with courage, determination and a will of steel
She finds the strength from deep within
Her love for him, will always win
To see beyond this broken shell
The strong young man she knew so well
A man once tall and strong and proud
Stood head and shoulders above the crowd
Now just a shadow of what he used to be
But this she knows, with such certainty
For better or for worse, in sickness and in health
Their love is unbreakable, it is their strength and wealth
His smile is beyond any treasure, worth more than any gold
And their love is more precious as they both grow grey and old.

Troubled Times

On the darkest night
You held me tight
From the very start
You held my heart
Through troubled times and raging storm
You kept me calm, safe and warm

A sanctuary for my fragile soul
My sorrow and fears you did console
Gently you held my hand
And helped me to understand
Eased my fears and calmed my mind
With words of comfort, compassion so kind

You lead me through the confusion and the haze
On my darkest hours and darker days
Safe from my sorrows, my worry and pain
Through the darkest nights and dreary rain
You kept my troubled nightmares at bay
Until the light of a brand new day.

Fly Away My Butterfly

Like a butterfly caught in the breeze
You said your dreams you had to seize
Those dreams, you said, did not include me
I could not hold you , so I set you free
But I had built my dreams around you
I thought our love was strong and true
But you said my love was just an illusion
Leaving me dazed and in a state of confusion
My hopes and dreams inside just died
They were built on foundations of foolish pride
But like castles floating in the air
I watched them fade and disappear
My hopes and dreams lay torn and tattered
My fragile heart left empty and shattered

As you left my world and walked away
You did not look back that fateful day
Taking everything that was precious to me
I knew right then that I would never again see
Your smile, your face or hear your voice
In Life and Love, we must make a choice
But life goes on and we have to let go
Life is like a river, it must move and flow
Over rapids rocks, pebbles and stones
Dancing to many different moods and tones
Under both clear blue and stormy sky
Or become bitter and stagnant and slowly die
And though it pained and hurt me so
I knew I had to let you go

Yet every time I see a butterfly....

Chasing Memories

A memory awakes like a glowing ember
As the mind tries so hard to remember
A flicker of memory buried so deep
Oh what secrets the soul does keep
Transient thoughts that tantalise and tease
Memories of sadness and some that please
They hint and whisper of a forgotten past
Fleeting,intangible and moving so fast

From a distant time,a different place
The image of a long forgotten face
Eyes that dance and sparkle like wine
Skin as smooth as silk so fine
Lips that glisten and dare to be kissed
All but forgotten and shrouded in mist
Words of truth left unspoken
A heart left wounded and heart broken

The old man lies there in his bed
Chasing thoughts around his head
A glimmer of recognition in those eyes so green
The ghost of a memory can just be seen
Shadows and sunlight play on the wall
As he tries to remember and recall
But everyday it ends the same
He still can not recall her name.

She came for him, one cold winter's night
Standing by his bed in soft moonlight
She smiled and kissed his brow so tenderly
And whispered in a loving voice so softly
Take my hand, come dance with me
And remember how we used to be
Those sparkling eyes, awaken his mind
A face so graceful, beautiful and kind

He remembers the first time he saw her face
And how she made his heart beat race
Those halcyon days when they first met
Alas so short, but no time for regret
That first shy glance
That first slow dance
That first love's kiss
Those sheer moments of bliss

One more sigh, one more breath
He crosses the line between Life and Death
And waiting there in the welcoming light
She reaches to embrace and hold him tight
As young and beautiful as the day she had to leave
Leaving him heartbroken and all alone to grieve
But their love remains forever and the same
Taking her hand, he whispers her name...

Another Fool

I should have known from the very start
That you would be the one, to break my heart
You held me captive from the moment we first met
Oh how could I ever forget
The first time I saw you standing there
Running your fingers through your long dark hair
The way you moved so gracefully
That shy half glance as you noticed me

I know now that I should have walked away
And I would come to regret this day
That sparkle in your eyes, that half smile
 Knowing that I could only resist for awhile
Holding me captive, almost hypnotised
The light in your eyes had me mesmerised
But you had me from that first half glance
I should have known better, but I asked you to dance

A prisoner to your beauty and feminine charms
I could have held you forever, in my arms
That smile, that look, those tempting lips
That rhythmic dance, the sway of your hips
As I held you close as we moved so slow
Afraid to hold you tighter, afraid to let you go
But alas, it was not to be
You could not share your love just with me

Like a honey bee, from flower to flower
Intoxicated by your seductive power
The heat of the hunt, the thrill of the chase
With your feigned innocence and Angelic face
To you, love was a one way street
A trail broken hearts lay at your feet
You soon lost interest in your prey
Another fool, broken hearted and cast away

A little give and a lot of take
A serious commitment you could not make
You needed more than I could give
But the lies and deception, I find so hard to forgive
A weaver of promises and intangible dreams
A victim of your deceitful and calculating schemes
So cleverly crafted, woven and concealed
Until too late, the truth revealed

So I had break free before it was too late
A moment longer I could not wait
My shattered dreams and illusions were beyond repair
And all my plans and hopes had turned to despair
Searching for that sacred place deep inside
To heal my broken heart, my wounded pride
Cocooned in my chrysalis, my Sanctuary
Reborn again, stronger and free.

Alshaad Kara is a Mauritian poet who writes from his heart. His latest poems were published in one Magazine, "parABnormal Magazine September 2022" and three anthologies, "Les gardeurs de Rêves", "Love Letters to Poe, Volume 2: Houses of Usher" and "20.35 Africa: An Anthology of Contemporary Poetry Vol. V".

Nickname

So many names in my thoughts,
Yet you are the only one in my mind.

Tell me why I cannot forget you,
My heart had nicknamed you as my heartbeat...

It had no choice to accept this reality,
Of unrequited pain.

Your name was my smile,
Now I have just nicknamed you as my sadness,

Please forgive me,
But my heart breaks each time it hears your name...

It had no choice to accept this reality,
Of unrequited pain.

So many names in my thoughts,
Yet you are the only one in my mind.

Rules of Love

The religion of love is the divinity of the heart.

It comes as a frightening desire,
But soon settles as an addictive need.

To like or to love is no decision to make,
Since the heart has to choose.

There's always a slight unrequitedness in the heart,
Since love is an incomplete story,
Till it is unconditional.

The virtue of relationships,
Is the enshrined love that abodes the art of loving the
    heart passionately.

Selflessness is the unique way to bloom love forever
Since the heart has not to choose whom to shower its
    heartstrings...

Love comes from the heart,
And drowns in the heart for forever...

The Duet of Angels

Light that fire in my heart...
The emotions and passion set on my lover,
Are the heart of my dreams.

Love takes the shape of two,
Just like the spirit of a heart.

Cherish those precious words that work,
Because they are in our minds as memories.

The flame that burns even more,
Are the candlesticks we both lit,
In the sake of our love.

A dreamland in a dreamworld,
Light the flames in our hearts.

The Encomium

Everyday I used to wake up with you by my side,
Such was my memory,
Kissing your forehead whilst you swiftly went into my
    arms.

I would play with your hairs whilst you played with my
    body hairs.
Silence reigned yet our souls merged.

That envy for love further flourished when you set out for
    my unconditional love.
You would sleep by my side during the day,
Only to look into my eyes after slumber,
Falling more in love than ever.

Till that passion of frenzy brought us to a standstill...
We were not made for each other,
We understood that we were part of one another for
    eternity.

Today, you wake up by my side,
Kissing my lips gently whilst you looked passionately in
    my eyes,
The abode of dreams.

Love Letters in Poetic Verse

The Lovers
William Powell Frith, 1855

Cynthia Bernard is a woman in her late 60's who is finding her voice as a poet after many decades of silence. A long-time classroom teacher and a spiritual mentor, she lives and writes on a hill overlooking the ocean, about 20 miles south of San Francisco.

Her poems have been published or are forthcoming in a number of journals and anthologies, including *Multiplicity Magazine, Persimmon Tree, Heimat Review, Passager Journal, Writing in a Woman's Voice, What is All This Sweet Work?* (an Anthology from Vita Brevis Press), *Your Daily Poem*, and *MockingOwl Roost*.

In January 2023, Cynthia began her studies in the Master of Fine Arts program at Lindenwood University, with a concentration in poetry.

Love Songs

My heart is writing the happiest of love songs to you,
    Beloved,
A symphony filled with joy,
A gentle ballad of warmth and ease,
A sweetly lingering aria about that moment when my
    hand finds yours,
A madrigal of pleasure in your arms, by your side,
An ongoing improvisation of delight.

Once Upon a Time

Once upon a time
I saw your pictures online,
read your profile,
glimpsed a brilliant mind, a tender heart,
and decided to write.
You had posted your profile
but - most illogically - weren't expecting any messages,
and it took you a while to respond…
almost as long as it took you
to captivate my heart.

Once upon a time
we walked by the ocean,
masks on,
distancing, more or less,
walking and talking in the ocean air,
until the end of our visit,
when we took off our masks,
you smiled,
and a warm sweetness
began blossoming in my heart.

Once upon a time
we walked by the ocean…
Then, twice upon a time,
unmasked, holding hands…
And since, many upon a times,
we walk by the ocean,
and in the forest,
and around the reservoir,
and at the Marina,
and up to see the tadpoles,
and through the snow…

Once upon a now,
let's walk again,
and let's keep walking together,
for always upon a time.

Moving In

Boxes and cases, packing, unpacking,
down the stairs from my place,
up the steps to yours.
It's a wonderful old house,
big, overlooking the ocean,
lots of windows, much history—
the two of you, happily, then you alone.
And now, us.

I have been a frequent visitor,
delighted to be here with you as our togetherness begins,
but, of course, polite, a guest,
tiptoeing around your past
in every room, on every wall, overflowing every closet—
your past, to be held gently,
to be honored and also, now, somehow, contained.

I have been tiptoeing, but no longer.
We need to live here, both of us, being us,
we need to breathe,
to dance on every inch of floor in every room,
need to stretch out, to sing,
sometimes to stomp loudly, other times to whisper,
need our own crannies to fill,
not just those in-between spaces on some of your
    shelves,
need peaceful silence on some days,
toe-to-toe electric sparks on others,
and everything in between.

So, we are beginning to find our way,
feeling into how we fit together, you and I,
emptying and filling—shelves, closets, walls—
learning to make room for what was and what will be.
You open up spaces for me, I move into them,
and both of us, together, find new spaces—
the veggies I'm growing on the deck
in the boxes you built,
the camelia I planted near the front door
spreading out on the trellis you attached to the wall,
flowers floating in bowls of water,
dinner at a table outside.
We're making new history
in this old house.
Our house.

Leaving

It's true that I can love you from anywhere
and I will love you today
while I'm here
when I leave
while I'm traveling
and when I arrive—
love, the sweetest background music,
accompanies me in all I do
and my heart knows nothing of distance—
but oh, Beloved, my body does,
my sometimes fierce, sometimes oh-so-tender body
that wants to reach out and find you
right next to me
or, at most, a few steps away.
My body, the animal of me,
that loves holding and being held,
that melts into our gentle times
and delights in our passion.
I will be leaving later today,
and that's fine,
I'm a rational adult with my own life,
and I value my independence,
and after all, I'll be back soon…
but my body, my body does not want to go.

God Speed
Edmund Blair Leighton, 1900

 **John Wiley** started out as a ballet dancer and turned to poetry when his knees finally gave out for good. His work has appeared in several journals including *Terror House Magazine*, *The Writing Disorder*, *Detritus*, and *Horror Sleaze Trash* (under a pseudonym). He lives in a California beach town and works in his wife's audiology practice.

Love Letters in Poetic Verse

Girl in the Full Metal Jacket

Don't look for an angel in the girl
who leaves blistered fingerprints on my back,
self-possessed by a personal demon,
this ink-sheathed, scar-savvy
girl in the full metal jacket -
she does a shot and I'm drunk,
plays with knives and I'm cut,
explodes and I'm burned --

but scars are cool,
and I'm desperate to wear her marks forever.

First published in Terror House Magazine, 2019

Flirt

The way she looks at me,
        then lights her cigarette,
                then looks at me again, says,

"Oh, yeah - I know *aaaall* about guys like you."

The way I look at her,
        throw back a shot,
                then look at her again, says,

"Oh, yeah? Prove it."

Love is Best

Love is best under colored-paper lantern light,
in courtyards of red brick, beneath trees
whose branches frame the full moon;
with mellow air, and mist that mellows
moon and colored-paper light.

But the moon set hours ago;
the lanterns are gone gray,
the bricks uneven;

but the night air -
crystalline.
And your dancing -
sure-footed.

I Wish

she's lean,
loose jeans
hung on hip bones,
bell-bottoms frayed
around bare feet,
tee shirt tied up, neat navel;
messy bun…
coming undone…

she pulls the pins,
drops the bun,
flares the hair,
and shreds me
with a smile that says,
"you wish"

Originally published in Terror House Magazine

Love Letters in Poetic Verse

The Dawn of Love
Thomas Brooks, 1846

Southern Arizona Press

Jerri Hardesty lives in the woods of Alabama with husband, Kirk, who is also a poet. They run the nonprofit poetry organization, New Dawn Unlimited, Inc. (NewDawnUnlimited.com). Jerri has had over 500 poems published and has won more than 2000 awards and titles in both written and spoken word poetry.

Sensing

I indulge my eyes, cataloging the lines of your face,
Memorizing the sweep of your lashes, the curve of your mouth,
Secretly savoring your silhouette in the firelight.

Moving closer, I inhale the scent of you, catch my breath.
Heat and aroma rise together, slightly smoky, like the fire,
Permanent chemical imprints creating memories.

Your lips part, the honey of your voice filling the silence.
The sound of your speaking triggers shivering response in my spine,
Your words of love, the only thing for which I've ever lived.

Previously published in Mississippi Poetry Journal, 2011

Three Words

I love you.

Three small words,
Pathetic and inadequate,
Lacking even the sound
And fury
That signifies... nothing.

Three worn words,
Trite and overused,
Soiled words
Prostituted
To the service
Of millions of lips
Daily.

Three short words,
Incapable of crossing
That Great Divide
Between two beating hearts,
That Grand Canyon
Between two dreaming spirits,
Insufficient,
Falling, echo-less
From a leap
Evel Knievel
Would never
Dare.

Three dry words
Which cannot hope
To describe
That riptide
In the mind,
That tidal wave
In the body,
That drowning pool
In the soul.

Three simple words
That belie the
Complexities,
The intricacies,
The paradoxical
Mysteries
That a million
Poets have never
Adequately put
On paper,
Or in song,
Or in their lives.

But we try.

It was like
I'd spent my life
Some waterless fish,
Gasping for air,
And upon meeting you...
Began to breathe.

You once said
That my love poems
Are always about
Your love for me.
Well, that's simple.
You see,
My love for you
Is a constant,
It is without question,
Without hesitation,
I do not wrestle
With it,
Or worry
About it,
Or struggle
Against it,
It simply IS,
Like respiration.

I write
About more
Enigmatic things.
My love for you
Is ordinary to me.
The miracle worthy
Of poetry
Has always been
The way that you love me.

Previously published in Poetry Society of Virginia Prize Poems, 2020

Creative Living

My life is interlocked through time with yours,
Our stanzas woven thick with metaphors,
A rubaiyat of tangled twining rhymes,
Like ever-lapping waves on sandy shores.

Creatively collaborating crimes
Of passion and of art, at least at times,
We elevate our lives to poetry
Where daily strains seem only pantomimes.

The pleasure and the love we share are free,
My favorite place, with you, and yours, with me.
Together we unlock the endless doors
That lead to boundless possibility.

Previously published in Pennsylvania Poetry Society Prize Poems, 2021

Lovesong

I was a melody,
A long line of notes
Forming a trail behind me,
Wandering along alone,
Sometimes major,
Sometimes minor,
But I knew something was
Missing.
I heard you
From a distance,
Your own tune
A perfect harmony
To mine,
And as we joined
Our song,
We each discovered
New scales, new keys
We'd never played before.
Oh, sometimes
There was discord,
Improvisations
Gone wrong,
But we always returned
To our original
Lovesong.

Previously published in Pennsylvania Poetry Society Prize Poems, 2016

The End of the Song
Edmund Blair Leighton, 1902

 **Thomas Zampino** lives in New York and been an attorney for nearly 40 years. He began writing poetry only recently. Some of his works have appeared in The University of Chicago's *Memoryhouse Magazine*, *Silver Birch Press, Bard's Annual 2019, 2020, 2021, and 2022, Trees in a Garden of Ashes, Otherwise Engaged, Chaos, A Poetry Vortex, Nassau County Voices in Verse,* and *No Distance Between UsI,* and *The Wonders of Winter*. His first book of poetry, *Precise Moment*, was published in 202. Brazilian director and actor Gui Agustini produced a video enactment of his poem *Precise Moment*. His second book of poetry, *synchronicity*, was published in 2023 by Southern Arizona Press.

He can be followed at:

https://thomaszampino.wordpress.com/

Just One Word

Sometimes, it's just one word.
Sometimes, it's just one kiss.
Sometimes, it's the silence.
Each holds the power
Each turns the key
   that can change
      everything –
Just as you
   did me.

Through Thirty-Five Years

Through thirty-five years
   it's become increasingly obvious
      that we were not two halves
         desperate to become as one,
      but rather two complete mortal beings
   who joined together, freely in love,
only to find along the way
   that we've made each other
      stronger,
         wiser,
            more loving,
               more miraculous
   than we ever could have imagined on our own.
Two instruments completely transformed
   through one extraordinary symphony.

You Have Always Known That

Passion can overturn the status quo
    while affirming the truth that binds it.
Passion can engage the folly of men
    while bidding them to seek peace.
But rare is the one who sees the truth
    who knows from whence it comes.
Passion is a song at home in the soul
    and a heart that cleaves to the wind.
You have always known that.

 **Lynn White** lives in north Wales. Her work is influenced by issues of social justice and events, places, and people she has known or imagined. She is especially interested in exploring the boundaries of dream, fantasy, and reality. She was shortlisted in the Theatre Cloud 'War Poetry for Today' competition and has been nominated for a Pushcart Prize, Best of the Net, and a Rhysling Award. Her poetry has appeared in many publications including: Apogee, Firewords, Capsule Stories, Gyroscope Review and So It Goes.

Find Lynn at:

https://lynnwhitepoetry.blogspot.com
https://www.facebook.com/Lynn-White-Poetry-1603675983213077/

Bury Me Deep

Bury me deep in the tall meadow grass
and bury me deep in your arms.
Lie with me here in the sun ripening flowers
where the blue of the sky hides the clouds.

Bury me deep in your cool white sheets
and kiss my eyes and my mouth.
And as the warmth of your body flows in to mine
I'll bury you deep in my arms.

Oh, bury me deep beneath darkening skies
and hold me close to your heart.
And buried deep with our love complete
we'll sleep covered over in stars.

But the future lies with us heavy and dark.
It has bitter sweet memories of now.
With the tastes of the past buried deep in our love
the tastes of the future are sharp.

I can see both the stars and the blackness of night,
the blindness and brightness of love.
The past and the future cast shadows of time
so bury me deep in your love.

And bury me deep in the tall meadow grass
and I'll bury you deep in my arms.
And lie with me here in the sun ripened flowers
where the blue of the sky meets the clouds.

First published in Quail Bell, February 2017

Don't Go

When I'm with you
I feel I am whole.
Captured and completed.
Engulfed by you.
When you kiss me
all my fears disappear
in the kiss.
Where do they go?
I don't know.
Do you wrap them round your tongue
and swallow them whole?
I don't know.
I only know the comfort
I feel, such peace.
So don't go.
Don't go.
Please,
don't
go.

First published by Stacey Savage, Ed, One Love Foundation, We Are Poetry, An Anthology Of Love Poems, 2015

Dreaming

There was a time when
I knew where to find you,
knew the places and spaces
you inhabited
in my dreams,
in my day
and night
dreams.
You would be waiting there,
waiting to be found,
waiting to come
to me
revealing your secrets.
Now it's harder to discern you,
to recognise your shape and form.
You are becoming fragmented and ephemeral,
floating forms in a damp mist of change
holding on tight
to your secrets
Don't pass me by.
I still want to know you
to discover you
to learn what you've become.

First published in Heretics, Madmen and Lovers, Quotable Poe, October 21, 2019

 **Tasneem Hossain** is a Bangladeshi multi-lingual poet. Her wanderings in other areas of literature include fiction, translation, academic pieces, columns, and op-eds. She writes in English, Bangla, and Urdu. Her writings appear in magazines, different dailies, and annual publications of different countries. To name a few: International Human Rights Art Festival 2022 Anthology: *Tyranny Unchained; Woman's Freedom,* Southern Arizona Press 2022 anthology *The Wonders of Winter, The Mocking Owl Roost (USA), Borderless Journal* (Singapore), *Discover Mississauga and More* - eBook (Canada), *Krishnochura* (United Kingdom), *EDAS Chronicle, The Dhaka Literature, An Ekushey Anthology, The Daily Star, bdnews24.com, The Daily Star,* and *Asian Age Online* (Bangladesh). Her publications consist of *The Pearl Necklace* and *Floating Feathers (poetry),* and *Split and Splice (article).* She recently published a collection of poetry, *Grass in Green,* with Southern Arizona Press.

She runs a project named *Life in Verses* where she conducts poetry writing workshops.
She completed her Masters in English Language and Literature in 1986 from Dhaka University.

She is the Director of Continuing Education Centre (human capacity development organization). As a training consultant her expertise lies in Communication Management and Language. She worked as faculty (English Language) in Chittagong University of Engineering and Technology. She also worked as newscaster, commentary reader, and radio jockey in radio Bangladesh for 10 years. She directed Shakespeare's play *A Midsummer Night's Dream.*

She resides, sharing time, between Bangladesh and Canada.

Endless Love

Beneath the cherry blossom tree stands she,
Her bright eyes shining like stars in the sea.
Pink cherry fairies dancing in the gentle breeze,
Fluttering heartbeat as the maiden nervously breathes;
She waits for her lover this time every year.
Last time she didn't meet him out of fear.
Suddenly time stopped as letters stopped to appear;
She waited still for her lover to reappear.

Today as she stands with freckled wrinkled cheeks,
The day seems darker and very bleak;
Stormy winds and high rising tide of the sea at its peak,
Snow white hair blows past the winds, she starts to
　　　speak.
She smiles as the shadow sways on the waves;
Hands lifted she advances to embrace…..

Spring Sojourn

Come my love, spring is here.
Not a single tree is bare.
The world around now is like a fair
Beauty abounds, this sight is rare.
Let's rush to the garden tree.
Give me a kiss, reel in true ecstasy!!!

Naked earth wears a colorful gown,
Winter now has lost its crown.
Goddess of nature has spread her sparkling wand of ray,
Giving birth to colors yellow, white, purple and red spray
Spring flowers - daisies, tulips and daffodils; cherry blossoms and all that is best.
Apples, strawberries and almonds bloom in full harvest.

Sun shines high, bright sunny breeze,
Gentle, soothing, chilly wind caressing cheeks
Iris blooms and the lazy redbud rose,
Snowflakes' snow petals with little green spots on the nose
Bursting fragrance sprinkling across the bushes through the plains,
Painting pictures of colors on the new green carpeted vales.

Delicate yet powerful smell numbing the lips,
Sighing remembering forgotten days of emotional bliss;
Smiling lovers recollecting mysterious secret trips,
Whispering, holding hands, strolling through the mist
Singing their tales, flying butterflies and bees,
Chirping hidden thrush in the bushes and trees.

Melodious cuckoos' song, echoes across the oceans and
    seven seas.
Flowering polash, shimul and krishnachura's ethereal
    beauty I miss.
Reminiscing all our meaningless lover's fights,
Emptiness surrounds spring's chilly nights
Spring into the world brings new life and joy,
The mysterious force of God's ploy.

Come! fly across the oceans and the seas,
Be with me to enjoy the season and its peace.
Painful days will end in ease,
Powerful passions and rhythm of heartbeats increase.
Spring is here, fulfill my dream,
Hold me tight and give me a kiss.

Be My Lover

We tied the knot on a fine beautiful day,
Tender glances exchanged every day;
Smiles and love blossomed night and day.

Slowly, romance slipped away,
With all the hustle and bustle of each day;
We forgot to look at each other as time passed away.

Tired and worn out in the bed we lay,
Thinking, awake, of the next day;
Seldom looking at each other as months and years
    dragged away.

Gazing at others and thinking,
How happy and beautiful are they!
Remember, they also think about us this way.

Let us not delay, as time hastens away;
Make our vows and pledges stronger,
As we brave out years of roughness away.

Smile at each other every single day.
Tenderly kiss and rekindle the romance as we play,
Bringing back the memories to make us sway;
Tremble with powerful emotions once again, as we gray.

Loving and holding each other in our arms,
Offering solace and soothing each other like a balm.

Let everyday be a Valentine's Day;
Be my lover till the end of my day.

Love Letters in Poetic Verse

Joan McNerney is originally from New York City and now resides in the dank woodlands of upstate New York. She has been the recipient of three scholarships. She has recited her work at the National Arts Club, New York City, State University of New York, Oneonta, McNay Art Institute, San Antonio and the University of Houston, Texas as well as other distinguished venues. A reading in Treadwell, New York was sponsored by the American Academy of Poetry. She was recently named the second place winner in Wilda Morris Challenge.

Published worldwide in over 35 countries. Her work has appeared in literary publications too numerous to mention. She has been awarded four Best of the Net nominations.

The Muse in Miniature and *Love Poems for Michael* are both available on Amazon.com and Cyberwit.net. Just released is a new title *At Work*. This collection shows colorful but realistic snapshots of working women and men in their daily lives.

I See You in Bright Colors

Eating red ripe watermelon
while searching verdant trees
for bluebirds flitting pass us.

Remembering how fields
of brilliant wildflowers
beguiled us as we inhaled
fresh mowed grasses.

You would smile fingering
purple passion leaves.

Your favorite hour when
wide awake you listened
to the sounds of dawn
calling all colors out to play.

We shared the calligraphy of
oceans watching orange sunsets
splash through waves.

No one else has ever evoked
such a shining palate as you.

Noontime

Perfumed berries
and new grass.

Beneath honey locust
through hushed woods,
we found a spring.

My feet throb over
hard pebbles. Threading
soft water the sun
dresses us in golden
sequins.

Wildflowers

Bobbing in open fields.
Two fabulous daffodils sprout
from your eyes. Falling dizzy in
love as o so lackadaisical
breeze tugs at shirt sleeves.

Again we are flushed in
warm love caress. Solar
energy orbiting billions of
grass blades. Hum hum
hummingbirds hurry hurry
pass us tripping giddy
in love.

 **Rhian Elizabeth** was born in 1988 in the Rhondda Valley, South Wales, and now lives in Cardiff. Her debut novel, *Six Pounds Eight Ounces*, was published in 2014 by Seren Books, and her poetry collection, *the last polar bear on earth,* was published in 2018 by Parthian Books. Her prose and poetry have been listed in various competitions and prizes and appeared in many magazines and anthologies, as well as being featured on Radio 4's PM programme. She was named by the Welsh agenda as one of Wales' Rising Stars - one of 30 people working to make Wales better over the next 30 years. She is a Hay Festival Writer at Work and Writer in Residence at the Coracle International Literary Festival in Tranås, Sweden.

cease fire

there will come a day when our hair is white
two tangled puffs of cloud rising from our armchairs
the clock ticking - life's timebomb - on the living room wall
the sound of pomegranates being pried apart
all our nights like this, apple crumble warm

we'll urge the cats to finish their dinners
the things that happened such a long time ago
unreachable cobwebs left in the far corner of the ceiling
we have forgotten the names of our favourite songs
and our sides ache only with laughter.

death of a sunflower

i meant it when i said
how special i think you are.
and, like the sunflowers
that continue and continue
to grow on the Tuscan fields,
summer after summer,
august after august,
you *too* will continue and continue.

each sunflower's life ends, of course,
as everything that begins must end
but not yet
not yet

let's just watch this beautiful thing,
this rising of thousands and thousands
of yellow miracles
from the dark soil below,
without asking questions.

it starts like this

you meet on the internet.
up until now you've thought
this sort of thing beneath you -
online dating is something only
desperate people do, the last resort
for those lacking the heart and the hutzpah,
the stomach and the suave,
to seduce *real* people,
in *real* life.
how awfully tragic to put yourself
on display like that, like a nearly
out of date packet of ham all sad and sweating
in the reduced section
of the internet fridge.

oh love me, *please*!

but against your better judgment

                  here
            you
      are
swiping
               and
               there
               she
               is,
                                  smiling.

**Dr. Richard M. Bañez** is a Filipino associate professor for the undergraduate and graduate teacher education programs at Batangas State University JPLPC-Malvar Campus. As an educator, he is primarily interested in the pedagogy of language and literature across basic and tertiary education levels that focuses on teachers and students' capacity to engage in dynamic curricular opportunities and experiences within the context of teaching and learning English as a Second Language (ESL). He is also a literary artist whose works have appeared in selected volumes of *Covid-19 Pandemic Poems* by Cape Comorin Publisher.

A Villanelle for Love and Marriage

We get pricked by the thorns of the roses red.
Challenges and tribulations testing our marriage,
We remain in love and have a life ahead.

We work until the night shift to provide bread.
For building a family is more than hoarding courage.
We get pricked by the thorns of the roses red.

There were times we had bruised our hearts till they bled.
By keeping, growing, and holding anger in our storage,
We remain in love and have a life ahead.

We reconcile our differences every night in bed.
Recalling our oath to fight for our love with rage,
We get pricked by the thorns of the roses red.

We understand our lapses and regain the romance that
    once had fled.
To nurture our feelings and protect from those wanting to
    disparage,
We remain in love and have a life ahead.

None could alter our love, I have pled.
Faithful relationship, we can always manage.
We get pricked by the thorns of the roses red.
We remain in love and have a life ahead.

Dear Self

You, my discouraged self
Don't think too hard
I know life is not easy.
You can't always get
What you want.

What with that sad face?
Don't be bothered
Life could get along
Just wait and be strong.

I know something
beautiful might happen
If you continue dreaming on
With you, I'm here to hold on.

Set your courage
We will be sailing
Beyond the paradise
Breaking those boundaries
To surpass the heights
Of your dreams.

Remember this.
You are the greatest
Gift that had been blessed to me
For I'll never know
What's life without you.

So spare me a smile,
Wipe the sadness from your eyes,
Believe in yourself
For I love you the way you are.

I will always be here to stay
And remind you
Of the greatness that lies
In loving yourself.

Hide and Seek

It's never too late
To play hide and seek for two
With love.

Let me take the seeker's role
I close my eyes
Counting one, four, three
Sensing every beat of your heart
Till we're thrilled and prepared for this chase.

There's no boundary
To which you'd rested your hiding place –
Remote, long-distance, or faraway
Boundaries are not obstacles
For I'm destined to find you.

Make this game challenging
Incorporate unthinkable tactics
To conceal your feelings same like mine
Camouflaging in mutual understanding
Would you keep on hiding?

It doesn't matter if we take turns
Exchanging roles in this exciting play
Nor get tired of the numerous twists
Completely changing the rules of the game.

This hide and seek for two with love
Will remain an enchanting adventure
Forever fascinating and magical
For I know at the end of the day
Still, we will be searching for each other.

Love Letters in Poetic Verse

Hide & Seek, Phil May, 1896

 **Mark Fleisher** has not been nominated for any prizes – let alone won any – and aside from two semifinal finishes has not triumphed in any contest. Despite these setbacks the Albuquerque writer and Air Force veteran soldiers on and has four books of poetry sitting on the shelves of friends and people he does not know. His work has appeared in online and print anthologies in the United States, Canada, the United Kingdom, India, Nigeria and Kenya. His words have appeared in three previous anthologies from Southern Arizona Press for which he is eternally grateful.

Come to My Dreams

Guardian of the night,
keeper of the dark
I ask a favor
Take her hand
calm her fears
lead her gently
to the depths
of my subconscious
where dreams dwell
Let her and I be together
in tender embrace
touching, kissing
till no longer apart

Previously published in the author's Moments of Time (Mercury HeartLink 2014)

The Best Time

My love and I walk along beaches of sand
stride for stride, sometimes hand in hand
pausing to glean a shell from the shore
or listen to the melody of the waves' roar

We watch in awe the golden circle of sun
proclaiming this glorious day is done
as its slips majestically into the sea
bringing a private twilight to you and me

Previously published in the author's Moments of Time (Mercury HeartLink 2014)

Into the Essence

Peer into my eyes
take my hand
trust me
Let us travel
not by plane or train
car or boat or any
mechanical means

Come via our hearts
to our inner essence
on a path we often walk
each time taking more steps
reaching deeper levels
A mystery, yes, but not
shrouded in darkness or fear
of where we go, what we find

No, the way is suffused
with light from love's beacon
shining upon the discovery
of what defines us
allows you to be you
allows me to be me
within our sacred togetherness

Previously published in the author's Moments of Time (Mercury HeartLink 2014)

 **April Garcia** was born and raised in South Central Texas, Garcia's passion for writing poetry began in high school. Her work has appeared in multiple anthologies published by the Laurel Crown Foundation of San Antonio, Texas, Southern New Hampshire University, and River Paw Press with an upcoming publication in the *Chaos Dive Reunion* anthology by Mutabilis Press. She was included in Northwest Vista College's literary journal *The Lantana Review* as well as a number of online literary magazines including *The Penmen Review*, *Red River Review*, and *Unlost Journal*. Her most recent work appeared in the November 2022 issue of *Voices de la Luna*. Garcia is a wife and mother now homeschooling four children. She earned her Bachelor of Arts in general studies majoring in poetry from Southern New Hampshire University. She is a member of The Poetry Society of Texas, and also enjoys reading, crocheting, hiking, blogging, and traveling.

Kisses from a Bottle

Journey to summer
one August
early morning.

Before sun
—broke.

Your unexpected hand
—inviting.

I did not escape.

Passion fueled
from wine.

Hunger driven
from a kiss.

So Much More

The sun beats off your hair,
your hazel eyes
—darkened skin.

You are strong.

Maybe you think it couldn't be anything at all,
or maybe you think it has to be something else.

(To tell you the truth, it's all the above—and more.)

You say what's on your mind,
you hold me when I'm sad,
you scold me—when I'm bad.

You'll only let me have my way,
if what I want seems fair.

Unholy Love

I run barefoot through night.
No breath
to release.

You—
Me—
An unholy union.

You are a creature of the night.

And I—
I am a child
of light.

First published in the Dreamcatcher 2009 anthology by the Laurel Crown Foundation of San Antonio, Texas.

Ram Krishna Singh, also known as R.K.Singh, has been writing for over four decades. He was born (31 December 1950), brought up, and educated in Varanasi. He has been professionally concerned with teaching and research in the areas of English language teaching, especially for Science and Technology, and Indian English Poetry practices. Until the end of 2015, he served as Professor of English at IIT-ISM in Dhanbad. Dr Singh has published 52 books, including poetry collections *God Too Awaits Light* (2017), *Growing Within/Desăvârşire lăuntrică* (English/Romanian,2017), *There's No Paradise and Other Selected Poems Tanka & Haiku* (2019), *Tainted With Prayers/Contaminado con oraciones* (English/Spanish, 2019), *Silencio: Blanca desconfianza: Silence: White distrust* (Spanish edition, Kindle, Spanish/English, 2021), *A Lone Sparrow* (English/Arabic, 2021), *Against the Waves: Selected Poems* (2021), *Changing Seasons: Selected Tanka and Haiku* (English/Arabic, 2021), *Covid-19 And Surge of Silence/Kovid-19 Hem Sessízlík Tolkînî* (English/Tatar, 2021), and *白濁: SILENCE: A WHITE DISTRUST* (English/Japanese, Kindle Edition/Paperback, 2022). His haiku and tanka have been internationally read, appreciated, and translated into several languages. Dr Singh's haiku is also anthologized in *The Stars and Moon in the Evening* Sky (Southern Arizona Press, 2022). His awards and honors include Ritsumeikan University Peace Museum Award, Kyoto, 1999, Certificate of Honor and Nyuusen Prize, Kumamoto, 2000 and 2008, Lifetime Achievement Award of the International Poets Academy, Chennai, 2009, Prize of Corea Literature, South Korea, 2013, Aichi Prefecture Board of Education Award, Japan, 2015, Naji Naaman's Literary Prize, Lebanon, 2015, nomination for Pushcart Prize, 2013, 2014, and Citation of Brightest Honour, International Sufi Centre: Sufi World, Bangalore, September 2020.

More at: https://pennyspoetry.wikia.com/wiki/R.K._Singh. email: profrksingh@gmail.com.

Fount of Poetry

I seek new strides
in each of your moves
new dreams in your eyes and thighs

nude lyrics in lips
shape the night's sway
set my heart afire

I seek the lingering fragrance
the rhythm that frenzies the soul
the timeless joy you conceal

I seek the hues that blaze being
and shade the nest I rest in:
your chains renew freedom

each time I look at you
I see natural woman
the fount of poetry

Published in his collection of poems Sense and Silence: Collected Poems (Jaipur: Yking Books, 2010)

 **Doug Croft** is a community development leader and not-for-profit fundraising director. He journals poetically and writes occasional essays or short stories. Croft has multiple publishing credits in various anthologies and journals. He has received two awards in regional writing competitions and has written five sketches which were performed at business events. His chapbook, *Nature*, was published in 2022 and his first full-length poetry collection, *Exposed Roots*, is slated for publication in early 2023. Croft lives in North Carolina from where he works, writes, hikes, spends time with his two adult children, and travels to see as many of his favorite rock 'n' roll bands as possible.

Your Beautiful Heart

What is the way
To your beautiful heart
Is it wine, flowers and song

If I promise to love
And deliver above
Will that bring your heart along

Might I whisper to you
In soft voice anew
The beauty which I behold

Or should I shout it out loud
Proclaiming that I am proud
Announcing my love so bold

Will you give to me
Vulnerability
Which I will treasure with care and hold

In loving so free
Sharing pleasure with glee
We both can cherish and hold

If I could earn
Your beautiful heart
I would do all of these and more

I'd commit and promise
And live accordingly
For ever more

I Love You

When I am lost
You are my anchor

When I need to love
It is you to whom I give

When I wish to be surrounded by beauty
I peer at you, enraptured by your ravishing loveliness

When I desire softness in this hard world
It is your luscious features which I gently caress

When I seek purpose in my life
I love you

Love Letters in Poetic Verse

S Afrose (Sabiha Afrose, from Bangladesh) has been writing since Aug-2020.

Her works have been published in magazines and anthologies.(as for example.- *Spotlight, Dancing with Death, Women the Society Backbone, Inked with passion, Perception, Quintessence* etc.) She loves to read and write. She has been writing in different pattern whether poetic arts or short stories, by using her imaginations and perceptions (English or Bangla). The motto is to spread inspirational words towards all people, for leading a lively life on earth.

In this writing world, she has achieved many certificates from renowned platforms with the Doctorate in Literature from Instituto Cultural Colombiano.

Her first e-book is *Spirits, Lively Life* (Prodigy Published USA)

Her first published poetry book is *Thanks Dear God* (Evincepub Publishing House, India; available on Amazon, Flipkart, Bspkart, Evincepub.com). Her second book is *Poetic Essence* (Poetry Planet Publishing House, Philippines; available on Amazon, Bookemon), Her third book is *Reflection of Mind* (Ukiyoto Publishing platform, available on www.ukiyoto.com.) , Her fourth book is *Artistic Muse* (Literoma Publishing House, India). Her fifth book is *Glittering Hopes* (Ukiyoto Publishing Platform)

Apart this, she has published four Bangla poetry books and two English books in Bangladesh.

Her educational credentials are a B Pharm, M Pharm from Jahangirnagar University, Bangladesh. Her mother is Selina Begum and father is Manirul Islam. She lives with her beloved family.

She can be reached at :
afrosewritings@outlook.com or sabiha_pharma@yahoo.com

My Love

How many times
I will say dear
I love you so much
But you don't believe that.

You are my life
You are my spirits
You are my earth
You make my paradise.

Without you
I'm nothing
I can't be alive
I need your unconditional love.

Go dear dove
Spread my love
The azure's canvas
Will be my pride.

There I will make
My heart for your lovely life
Will you see
Pls believe me dear.

I can't imagine any moment
Without your smile
You make my shiny art
You're in my heart.

Oh dear God
Can't You help
Pls bless once more
I want to be with my beloved.

I know You will
Because You also love
Eternal flower is my dear
Heaven showers petals upon my earth.

 **Matt J. McGee** writes in the Los Angeles area. His poem, "Comrade With a Shovel" recently appeared in Southern Arizona Press anthology *The Poppy, a Symbol of Remembrance*. When not typing, he drives around in rented cars and plays goalie in local hockey leagues. He has Pru Pellar to thank for a lot of good ideas and late night salads.

It Happened the Night You Sneezed

Once a twin set of ropes to pull men in
your eyes were puffy, swollen, mildly red,
and your mouth - whose tongue could tempt
any dollar bill from a club-goers empty pocket
hung slightly open, almost gasping as the flu
rocked a body that had rocked worlds.

Your posture, usually upright to display
the surgically-enhanced gift you'd given,
slumped instead against the car door, ready to
tumble onto the roadway and right into bed,
where a few cats and maybe some hot soup
and television would be a night's repose.

The car windows were up, sealed. A few others
had rode in that very seat, and with the lightest sniffle
I'd cracked a window to let the vacuum take away
whatever disease they'd brought to the party. But us,
that night we incubated, as we have for years,
hatching a moment of unconditional love.

 **Connie Carmichael** is a former mental health care worker. She is retired and lives in Columbus, Ohio with her wife, her loyal dog, and a head full of poetry. Her poetry has been published in *Better Than Starbucks*, *Pocket Lint*, *Writers and Readers Magazine*, and *Open Skies Quarterly*.

The Kiss

It had been 103 years since he had been kissed
and I couldn't say what possessed me to do it.
I kissed the three fingers between my thumb and little
    finger
and pressed them against his forehead.
It felt warm from the April sun.
He thought it was a cricket.
This time, I kissed my fingers
and planted them firmly against his cheek.
He smiled and the wind tickled the grass around his feet.
The dust from an army of trees fell from gnarled
    branches,
danced across the top of his head
and slowly trickled into the grooves of his name.
I left him lying in his bed, above the river and below the
    sky,
whistling through the dust and waiting for another kiss.

 **C. A. MacKenzie** writings are found in numerous print and online publications. She writes all genres but invariably veers toward the dark —so much so her late mother once asked, "Can't you write anything happy?" (She can!)

She published her first novel, *Wolves Don't Knock,* in 2018, and *Mister Wolfe (*the darkly dark second) in 2020. Two volumes of grief poetry commemorate her late son Matthew: *My Heart Is Broken* and *Broken Hearts Can't Always Be Fixed*. She has also published other books of poetry and short story compilations, all available on Amazon or from her.

Cathy divides her time between West Porters Lake and Halifax, Nova Scotia, Canada.

She can be followed at http://writingwicket.wordpress.com

Love Letters in Poetic Verse

Flowers of Love

You send me flowers for Valentine's,
cut flowers, colourful and fragrant,
beautiful—
and they brighten up the room
and my day,
but they soon die:
they wither and dry,
their leaves brown and
petals darken
and fragments fall to the floor.

Yet...

They can be pretty
as dried flowers,
and if you don't touch them
they won't shatter and turn to ash.

We can be like flowers—
strong one day,
fragmented the next—
when we are touched by life and time,
but we will endure,
our two lives will exist as one
whether we are together or apart,
for we were meant to be
like perennial blooms of flowers.

Previously published in One Red Rose, Dancing With Bear Publishing, February 2012.

Southern Arizona Press

To My Future Valentine

My love for you, my partner dear,
Will be given without fear,
I know I don't know you yet
As I'm still looking—we haven't met,
But our love, strong and demanding,
Will be forever and longstanding,
And on that glorious day when we do meet,
When finally each other we do greet,
My love will be given to embrace
And sweetness will shine upon your face,
You waited so long for me to appear,
You will always be so dear.

Previously published in One Red Rose, A Valentine's Day Anthology, Dancing With Bear Publishing, February 2012.

 **Jackie Chou** is a poet residing in Southern California who has work published in *Rat's Ass Review*, *Alien Buddha Zine*, *Spillwords*, *Fevers of the Mind Poetry Digest*, *Highland Park Poetry*, and others. She holds a bachelor's degree in Creative Writing from the University of Southern California. Besides writing, she loves to watch Jeopardy and talent competitions like The Voice.

Formosa

Your breath awakens me
to an isle of swaying palms
and loosed ankles.
You dance in the shadows
of crisp-winged butterflies,
auspicious like a yellow kitten,
prodding your ideologies into my head,
your brown hair tousled in the breeze,
ambition glowing in your pupils.
Your musical notes cross my stave,
your fingers bent at the right angles,
holding chopsticks with dexterity,
in night markets of neon boulevards,
where omelets are flipped and mice thrive,
your eyes locking with mine,
in our shared landscape.

Love Poem

This is not the kind of poem
where I put you on a pedestal
like a cold stone statue of Adonis

Nor is it some sort of superhero fantasy
where I watch you soar
from high-rise buildings
in a tight bodysuit with a cape

Rather, it's the kind of poem
where our souls unite
as I lay my head on your chest
listening to the beats
of your sentient red heart

In Bed, The Kiss
Henri de Toulouse-Lautrec, 1892

**Emily Bilman, PhD** is a poet-scholar who lives and writes Geneva, Switzerland. Her dissertation, *The Psychodynamics of Poetry: Poetic Virtuality and Oedipal Sublimation in the Poetry of T.S. Eliot and Paul Valéry,* with her poetry translations, was published by Lambert Academic in 2010 and *Modern Ekphrasis* in 2013 by Peter Lang, CH. Her poetry books, *A Woman By A Well* (2015), *Resilience* (2015), *The Threshold of Broken Waters* (2018), and *Apperception* (2020) were published by Troubador, UK. "The Tear-catcher" won the first prize in depth poetry by The New York Magazine. Poems were published in *Deronda Review, The London Magazine, San Antonio Review, The Wisconsin Review, Expanded Field, Poetics Research, The Blue Nib, Tipton Poetry Journal, North of Oxford Journal, Otherwise Engaged Magazine, Literary Heist, The High Window, Wild Court, Remington Review, Book of Matches, Lothlorien Poetry Journal, Poets Live Anthology 4, OxMag, San Diego Poetry Anthology, Contemporary Poetry 2022, Ballast Journal, Soren Lit, Southern Arizona Press Anthologies, Poetry Salzburg Review.*

She blogs on her website:
http://www.emiliebilman.wix.com/emily-bilman

Love's Reply

World-weary, the poet returned from
His pilgrimage and longed for his absent
Other-half with his young heart whose core
He could not reach: his reason was obscured
By doubt. He was muddled up and tired.
In the garden, he picked a dappled autumn
Rose whose thorns hurt him. To the poet
Whose head was bent in melancholy,

Love replied: "You heart is rent. Your other-
Half was ill. Love healed her by offering her
Your heart. Love is but a flower whose pistil
Is hidden like your own self inside your inner being
So you can abandon yourself and perceive
Your other-half as your consolation."

Published in Apperception, Matador, United Kingdom, 2020.

Initiation

You said the taste of the salmon eggs
On toast we had remained in your mouth

After we parted. You said you missed me.
A month later, you were forever gone.

You died suddenly like the juvenile fox
You gunned down in our nocturnal garden.

After your death, my muteness accompanied
The lead-silence that invaded our house.

Your absence felt like a broken metaphor
Whose figure of weakness was devoid of its vehicle.

Yet, your ghost-shadow constantly remained
With me like a companion in waiting.

While the sky turned crimson pewter-grey,
The doves flew off from the scented bower.

As I journeyed towards Ithaca, unafraid
Like Ulysses of the rough seas ahead,

I unraveled my secret quest of self-discovery
Deeper than the deepest ocean trench,

Sustaining like the lustrous salmon eggs
We ate during our last meal together.

Published in Apperception, Matador, United Kingdom, 2020.

Love Letters in Poetic Verse

The Whispering of Love
William-Adolphe Bouguereau, 1889

Dvora Robinson lives in Portland, Oregon, with her husband and their cat, Meeps. She holds a BFA in Printmaking and has worked as a Library Tech in academic libraries. In addition to writing, she likes to make visual art, swim in rivers, take walks, and spend time with friends. Her short poem "Powell Butte" can be found on buses in Vancouver, Washington, as part of their Poetry Moves project.

Your Skin as Warm as a Rock

Your skin as warm as a rock baking in the sun,
your lips the cool of the river rushing by,
the arc of your rib cage swooping
down to your tender belly,
my hand on the smooth skin,
moving clockwise, round and round,
the unfaltering thump thump under your sternum,
the steady puffs of your breath,
your eyelids flickering, chest rising and falling.
Oh furry chest, oh full lips, oh wide expanse of ribs,
oh the supple heat of your skin,
oh the weight of your leg over mine,
steady thumps, steady rise and fall,
sturdy rib cage, heated drum of a belly,
my hand hypnotized by its own circling motion,
soft hairs on your belly, wiry hairs on your chest,
stiff hairs in your beard,
my hand circling, your lips cool, your exhales
soothing "pah's" across full lips,
the steadfast rise and fall, rise and fall,
thump, thump, thump.
All this and skin and heat and sturdy
and oh, the perfection of this moment,
lulling me to sleep, your presence
the enveloping sweetness I long for.

The Siren
John William Waterhouse, 1900

Shirsak Ghosh is a State Aided College Teacher at Serampore Girls' College, West Bengal, India. He is a faculty member of this college for a few years. Besides teaching, which is his profession, he composes some creative poems. He has composed some poems published in following journals like IJELLH, Literary Herald, Literary Cognizance and GNOSIS. Some of his poems were published in different edited books like Aulos: An Anthology of English Poetry, Insulatus: An Anthology of Modern English Poetry, Otherwise Engaged: A Literature and Arts Journal, Contemporary Visions: An Anthology of Poems and COVID-19: Impressions on Society. He had recently published his poem in Indian Periodical.

Close Encounters

Looked, at me, blankly inscrutable over the phone,
Those rancorous words struck amiss belligerently
Left a surly expression in my soul
That unquenchable fire cannot ever be cured.
Eyes burned with anguish; face became paler.
Anger flamed in my heart, but a pang of larger guilt tore me
Into several pieces of hatred.
Gladly suffered in silence; despair never allowed
My emotions show, even when matters concerned me so deeply.
It was like a whiff of smoke, leaving behind a distastefulness
That's extremely hard to dismiss.
Nothing can placate and douse the inner irrepressible fire
Of those retorted expressions thus enlightening a frisson of horror
Within this tempestuous soul. To sabotage this inner demon of my mind,
The soul recalled those breathtakingly beautiful moments
When She played a pivotal role in my life. Forgave and wished her
The best in all aspects of her growth in her life.
The soul could not cry but can visualize her crying her eyes out
Which cannot be seen unless felt at an arm's length silently!

Penning through excruciate pedestrian poetry,
This agonizing soul can connect with her and pray for her honestly
She can only discover her truest self
And fixed her gaze, free from worries and liberation
Through her amazeballs looking glass.

Abaelard und Seine Schülerin Heloisa
(Abelard and his student Heloisa)
Edmund Blair Leighton - 1882

 **Adrian Ernesto Cepeda** is the author of *Flashes & Verses… Becoming Attractions* from Unsolicited Press, *Between the Spine* from Picture Show Press, *Speaking con su Sombra* with Alegría Publishing, *La Belle Ajar & We Are th Ones Possessed* from CLASH Books and his 6th poetry collection *La Lengua Inside Me* will be published by FlowerSong Press in 2023.

He lives with his wife in Los Angeles with their adorably spoiled cat Woody Gold.

Real Intimacy

Through realized
mundanity glimpse

insights sharing
a shape, peel

the person, butter
drip, bare, tell me honey,

press the magic
revel seeing the

beauty of the mundane,
you reveal me

through the ordinalities
discovered through

the flexibility savoring
every bite of sunshine

cooking in bed, mingled
silk intimate sheets

intermingling comes
the gravitational sun kissed

body stirring ingredients,
details blissfully laying

Love Letters in Poetic Verse

the mingled ripe primavera—
real intimacy overflowing

a burst into hibernation,
blushing the touch of our life.

Cento poem from Eve Lionheart's "on the intimacy of the mundane" from Medium.com March 21, 2021

 **Cai Quirk** is a trans and genderqueer multi-disciplinary artist who focuses on the intersection of gender diversity throughout history, its erasure, and contemporary reclamation and re*story*ation. Their self-portrait series '*Transcendence*' engages with connections between gender, mythology, and nature-based spirituality, and will be published this winter with Skylark Editions (presales available on skylarkeditions.org). In the last seven months, Cai has given over fifty talks and workshops in conferences across America, and their work was exhibited in five photo shows in October 2022 alone, in three states and two countries. In the spring of 2022 Cai received the *Minnie Jane Scholarship* and a four-month artist residency from the Pendle Hill Quaker Center. They received bachelor's degrees in music and photography from Indiana University.

See more at caiquirk.com.

Iridescent Silver

around you
I can be
my full
iridescent
self

shimmering
in every
color
beyond
the rainbow

surrounded
by waves
of
celestial
silver

shining
glorious
radiant
and
free

your silver
does not
chain me
or make
a cage

my full
iridescent
self
is
a butterfly

your silver
does not
pin me
to museum
displays

instead
I can roam
free
and here you are
alongside me

a silver-tongued
tech geek
flying on
wires and
guitar strings

our wings
and strings
make music
as we hum
our song

shining
together
in a
beautiful dance
around the sun

The Abduction of Psyche
William-Adolphe Bouguereau, 1895

Erica Ellis is a freelance editor living in Florida with her husband and two cats, having already launched two children into adulthood. She enjoys writing poetry and songs, walking on the beach, and no longer living somewhere where it snows. She worked as a veterinary technician, a dolphin trainer, a sea turtle researcher, and a wildlife biologist before finding her way to editing, though it should have been easier, as she has loved words and writing since she was a child. She hopes to keep writing until she is an old lady, preferably surrounded by cats.

Entire Nation

You are my entire nation

I need no other roads
than those
   that crisscross your heart
   and snake across your thighs

No other land
  than your body
sometimes rich fertile soil in which
  I dig my fingers deep
sometimes rocky cliffs that give
 no purchase

You are my East
my West
the coast upon which I stand
to look toward unknown places
to reach for different air
the plains to which I retreat
when that air becomes too thick
too full of strangers
and always my North
the steady point that allows me
to wander
and draws me back
to our truth

You speak to me in
   our own language
your tongue sometimes
tripping over the syllables,
a word from the dead language of a past love
occasionally sneaking across the border
of your lips
a fugitive
an outlaw

But when we whisper to each other
at night
in the dark
it is song
poetry
the stories of Scheherazade
saving my life

You are my entire nation

You are my Florida
   salty sweat
   as we pull ourselves
   through the humid atmosphere
   of our sex

You are my California
   rare golden light
   everyone's longing
this love, mine
But the ground of it
   sometimes shakes
   and gapes
   and swallows me

You are my Minnesota
   biting cold
   that steals the air
   from my lungs
but finally gives way
   to a fragile warmth
   that heats the nascent forgiveness
   lying fallow in my heart
melts the ice I have grown
   across my face
   to keep you from
   my waters

You are my Carolina
   the low murmur of waves
   crashing on some distant shore
when I need
myself and only
myself
And the shrieking song
   of a summer swarm
   of cicadas
when we find each other
in our joy

You are my entire nation

my roads
my fields
my forests
my mountains
my oceans

The map of which
I will spend
my whole life
learning

Galileo

I don't want to love you
like Galileo
and his stars

on the other side of the looking glass
and always
the dark
and the days
between

I don't want to love you
like an explorer
on the sea
Columbus or Magellan
looking always
in the distance
longing for a glimpse
of brown and green
hanging on the promise
of the scent of grass

I want to love you
today
this minute
here
now

I want to feel your skin
beneath my hands
Taste your saltiness
on my tongue
Breathe in the smell
of mowed grass
and Dial soap
and this morning's coffee
as you kiss me

I want to love you
today
this minute
here
now
Like a child
digging in the dirt
Whose whole world becomes
the patch of ground
in front of her
No thought of
muddy knees
or dinner bells
or why
Lost in the feel of
fingers
digging deep
into the earth

I want to love you
today
this minute
here
now

Like a mother
nursing her baby
in the darkness
Watching moist pink lips
grabbing hold
Feeling the tug
of mouth
on nipple
Understanding
how God
must have felt
on that sixth day

Surprised to hear
the birds begin to sing
and to see
a faint hint of purple
in the sky
to realize that
time hadn't stopped
for anyone
but her

I want to love you
today
this minute
here now

In this bed
In this house
With this breath
On this day

And again...
.................tomorrow

Allan Lake is a poet, originally from Allover, Canada, who now writes in Allover, Australia. Coincidence.

His latest collection, *My Photos of Sicily*, was published by Ginninderra Press contains no photos, only poems.

No Secret Anymore

Sent a song to a married woman today.
It'll trouble her but at least I'm consistent,
up close or at considerable distance.
'Secret Love', the Ry Cooder version.
People usually move on after divorce.
We did, in all the measurable ways.
Sold the home. Divided, split, moved.
Never bump into each other now.
Adult kids (fruit of our bumping) make
sure of that. We both repartnered –
other people of course – years ago.
A friend of mine married/divorced
same person twice! I wouldn't inflict
myself on anyone more than once.
Anyway, love went to seed, felt
tired but it never actually expired.
Just wanted her to know
that I know.

Laurice E. Tolentino is an Instructor at Batangas State University TNEU JPLPC-Malvar, Philippines where she instructs Professional and General Education courses for programs in College of Teacher Education as well as Major subjects for programs in International Hospitality Management. For the past two years, she has served as the College of Teacher Education's research coordinator and most recently in-charge as Food Services at the same university. In addition, she spent the full year serving as the Faculty Advisor for the Junior Hotelier and Restaurateur Association's (JHRA) from (2008-2010, 2016-2018 & 2020-2022). From 2016 to 2020, she worked as an OJT Coordinator for IHM Students. Within her personal life, she has a strong interest in advancement and self-development. She is constantly looking for fresh challenges and chances to pick up new skills that express her values for learning new things and for improving oneself.

Parental Love

A world dedicated to mothers and sons.
I want you to understand your worth and value.
You got all you deserved, and that's all I wanted for you.
I wished for you to have happiness, love, and a place where you belonged.
I am certain I have given you all I have worked so hard to provide.

I am not a man, though.
I have no idea how to shave a beard, fix cars, or toss a football.
I can only share your grandfather, who is also my own father, with you.
A man who has shown me honesty, wisdom, and consideration.
A man who has demonstrated male love in the most admirable way possible.

But I still have to say I'm sorry.
I'll be here for you no matter what, I swear to you.
My promise to you is not that I will love you as a mom and a dad,
but as a mom with the heart of both.
My promise to you that everything will be OKAY.

Independency

She is a mother of one child.
With a lot on her mind
She is resilient and self-reliant.
That is very difficult to find.

She consistently gives it her all.
to maintain a lovely home.
I understand that it's difficult for the two of us.
But somehow, we'll manage to make it through.

She is strong.
She doesn't ever leave.
She faces problems.
But she gives it her all.

Love Letters in Poetic Verse

Mother and Child in the Garden
Herbert Blande Sparks, 1916

 **Dr. Sara L. Uckelman** is an associate professor of logic and philosophy of language at Durham University. Her short stories, poems, and art are published or forthcoming in *Last Leaves*, *Manawaker Studio Flash Fiction Podcast*, the *Martian Wave*, *Pendemic.ie*, *Pilcrow & Dagger*, *Speculatief*, *Story Seed Vault*, *Sylvia*, *Tree & Stone*, and *With Painted Words*, and anthologies published by BCubed Press, Black Hare Press, Exterus, Flame Tree Publishing, Grace & Victory, Hic Dragones, Jayhenge Publications, QueerSciFi, and WolfSinger Publications. She is also the co-founder of the reviews site SFFReviews.com, and founder of the small press Ellipsis Imprints.

Nequeo, Nequis, Nequit

I cannot,
I cannot, I cannot
contain the words within,
catch the feeling, watch
the sunlight burst
on your face again,
I cannot turn away.

You cannot
seem to see me, hear the
words, bursting forth from
within, *nequeo nequis nequit*
it cannot, it cannot be
that I should falter
and fail, that you should pass
by, that you cannot feel the
line between us, tugging,
it cannot be just
my imagining, it has
to be real.

This cannot be anything
other than real.

"and in the compound nequeo, nequis, nequit ("I cannot, you cannot, he/she/it cannot")."

 **Douglas M. Lynn** has been married for 45 wonderful, happy years. Forty-five out of 50 plus isn't a bad average. I am a professional "wordsmith." He has had the opportunity over the last 48 years to speak to assemblies great and small (mostly small) about 3,500 times. He is a certified counselor, life coach, and mental health coach. Their only child lives in Mesa, Arizona while he currently lives in Ohio. He informed his son-in-law before they were married that he didn't want to be a burden to him when he got older - but he would. He is working on that prophetic utterance. He is also working on the "wonderful and happy" part of marriage.

Angel of Love

Why should one, such as I, be blessed with an Angel of Love?
There are many other men who are far worthier of such a prize.
Yet...I find myself to be in possession of a rare treasure from above.
Why the am I the chosen one? A test? Ah yes, a test I surmise.

If she be a test of some sorts, then what is my goal?
Is it to conquer the world or find some bird of peace? A dove?
Or is it that I'm to save the world from burying itself in a hole?
I think it's to give my all, my heart and soul, to my Angel of Love.

Could it be that this angel, this Angel of Love is a mortal?
Nay, I say to you that she is far from being so,
For her being radiates with kindness as if flowing from an heavenly portal.
How could one so beautiful and fair be anything from here below?

If by some queer fate or miracle of God I live to be one thousand and one,
I will dedicate each day, yea even each minute, to my Angel of Love.
Or if I pass from this world into another from lost time spun,
I pray that God will once more favor me and guide me to my Angel of Love.

 **LindaAnn LoSchiavo** is a native New Yorker. She has been nominated for a Pushcart Prize, Rhysling Award, Best of the Net, and Dwarf Stars. She is a member of SFPA, The British Fantasy Society, and The Dramatists Guild. She was an Elgin Award winner. *A Route Obscure and Lonely*, *Concupiscent Consumption*, *Women Who Were Warned*, Firecracker Award, Balcones Poetry Prize, Quill and Ink, and IPPY Award nominee *Messengers of the Macabre* [co-written with David Davies], *Apprenticed to the Night* [Beacon Books, 2023], and *Felones de Se: Poems about Suicide* [Ukiyoto Publishing, 2023] are her latest poetry titles.

Love Letters in Poetic Verse

Valentine Villanelle

Although I've made it holy in my mind —
Our sweet hypnotic love, my fantasy —
That place I left by your side was not mine.

Confounding me with sounds my heart refined,
Unsteady dreaming fanned hyperbole.
(Instead I've made it holy.) In my mind,

Stored, polished memories of us still shine,
Attaching me to what was not to be.
That place I left by your side wasn't mine.

Love's air is thin. Love's words breathe hard, designed
To signify rich unreality —
As though I've made it wholly in my mind.

She drinks you dry, so here you are, inclined
Towards me, embracing chance illegally.
That place I left by your side wasn't mine.

My parents named me for Saint Valentine.
A martyr's passion is his ecstasy.
But though I've made you holy in my mind,
That place I left by your side wasn't mine.

Twilight in Italy with Phoenix
For D.H. Lawrence [1885 – 1930]

Forged phoenix half-forgotten, British bird,
Alert and cocked for one right word, consumed
By fever-flamed consumption, whose choked breath
Stopped prophecies that would deliver us.

Pale, white-paged peacock: manuscripts mailed out—
Brave, flammable prose burned and judged "obscene"
By cocksure hypocrites who'd never know
Might's heights, Lorenzo, fed on festive wine
Of illness's blood sherbet. You produced,
As coughing came not softly, work brighter
Than critics could enjoy wild, strangled sounds
You would find somewhere safe to land abroad,
Igniting souls, your pen no match for most.

Fools won't write you out. Bertie, lover, son.
You've blazed rainbowed earth. Books multiply,
My guardian guide, tutor by their wounds,
Consume us — red inheritance of loss.

Lovers in a Landscape
Nicolas Lancret, c.1736

 **Meaghan M. Murphy** is a PhD student studying Comparative Literature at Indiana University. She currently lives and works in Hangzhou, China where she attends poetry readings, climbs mountains, and practices her terrible Chinese.

Desperately and Silently, I Love You

Desperately and silently, I love you
Stranger beside me on the subway
In whose reflection I see my sister
Who is so much younger than you
And is sweet and silly and talks too much.
Unlike you, silent, tired, drifting into me
First as dark strands of hair, then
A head slowly dropping to my shoulder
And I know I cannot move or breathe or
Wake you, hold you, tell you about her.
Cannot do anything except sit and hope
That your stop will come before mine.
That I will not leave you here, heavy-eyed
And alone, under fluorescent lights.
And, most of all, praying that one day
When she is older, sits solitary and tired
A stranger beside her will hold so carefully still.

Today I Bring for You

Today I bring for you carved jades, beaten gold,
    turquoises, pearls, and five round red cherries
In return I ask very little
Only
A reunion with the rain
My lover
Whom I have missed these many days

Today I bring for you sweet persimmons, fine silk shirts,
    heaps of nutmeg and cinnamon and every kind of
    spice.
In return I ask very little
Only
An abatement from the heat
Which presses
Like a crowd against my sweating skin

Today I bring for you ancient scrolls and leather bound
    books, the pages of which contain every secret of the
    world.
In return I ask very little
Only
The vast vault of the sky
Filled up
With every color of cloud

Today I bring for you my self, my words and my gifts and
 my darting eyes with which I take in all of you.
In return I ask very little
Only
One single set of eyes
Which
Might also take me in

**Sakariyahu A. Jamiu** is from Western part of Africa, Nigeria. He is currently a student of University of Ilorin in the Department of English and Literary Studies. He writes poems that dwell with issues such as love, hatred, depression, freedom and of course, a lover of African Culture ,customs, and traditions. His artistic work of art has featured in magazine such as *Panache*, *The Raven*, and among others. With his love to create aesthetics in writing, he has written prose poetry like "Letter from the Dead", "The tommy diamond e.t.c.," and continues to write issues that is currently trending in the outer global environment.

Letter to the Treasure

The love I have for you is far beyond the horizon
Beyond the skies and clouds.
Very high beyond the summit of the Everest,
And the end of the beginning.

If I were to describe how much I love you,
I will use the sky as the paper,
The ocean as the ink,
The earth as the table,
And heaven as the chair,
Still, I will find them not enough.

Behold, glimmers of your eyes set the dark clear,
The whiteness of your teeth,
And the road between your *pots* catapults me
Into the giant land of senselessness.

I hope there is a day
I will wake up in between the earth and heaven of your
    chest
Smiling to the melodies that come within.
And
Beyond what world could tell
And
Beyond what my brains could sense

 **Donna Kathryn Kelly** is a poet, playwright, novelist, and attorney. Kelly practiced law for more than two decades, primarily in the Illinois criminal justice system. Kelly is the author of The Cheney Manning Series, a two-part novel series, featuring an Illinois public defender turned amateur sleuth, who solves crimes in the Fox River Valley area of northern Illinois. Kelly's poetry has appeared in The Mocking Owl Roost, Heart of Flesh, North Dakota Quarterly, Bowery Gothic, and Southern Arizona Press.

You can find Kelly on Instagram @donnakathrynkelly.

Dusk-Love Sonnet

Strong love, I dance with you at dusk's delight,
for day has stolen half-century's past.
For you, I wish to wrangle swift twilight,
and cause its too-brief beauty to outlast
the sun and moon, which it may cast aside,
but never the spell that you claim ensnared.
You, kindest heart – You, sweetest soul inside -
yours is October's chance whom fortune dared
to view even without a crystal ball,
the inscription of words upon your heart.
Mine is the pen with which I corral,
our deepest dreams to never part.
We now forge this most solemn relation:
You, my stars, my knight, my constellation.

The Day Before the Day Before Valentine's Day in Year Two of the Pandemic

At first neglect, I saw not your full face
Because it was concealed by whiskers -
Your voice, compared to others, a whisper -
Your heart, incomparable in its space.
Our lives, through divergent paths coalesce.
We kiss, in a garage full of winter.
Our love, tested as such, shall not splinter,
Nor shall passion, despite time, deliquesce.
You, mumbling man with such a sweet soul;
I collide with you in words, in you with warmth,
Safe in your arms, secured by faithfulness,
Even the fire of pandemic you cajole,
With strength and steadiness you reassure;
For this, my love, my heart, my gratefulness.

Gitanjli Mridul is a poet and teacher from India. She earned a Masters' degree in English Language and Literature. She is a hilly woman from the beautiful hills of the Himalayas and writes in her native language of Hindi as well as English. She is a nature-loving poet.

Soul Baring

O my sleeping prince
I'll wait till you open your beautiful eyes
You don't know how much I waited
It was eons wait with desperate longings
In the desert of my sanguine heart
I kept an oasis hidden for you
Lest the merciless time should kill
And crumble
the hidden petals of my oasis!

O my prince
My wait has planted more beautiful
Flowers in my oasis!
How fruitful is the patience
How futile is the anxious anxiety
I welcome thee to shower in the fragrance
Of my sandalwood pasted bare body
This sacrificial altar I adorned
For my prince charming
For you only!

Oh ! You are so sleepy!
Tired of your journey to find
Your destination ! your waiting princess
Oh! I must lick clean your sweat
Those precious pearls pristine
Your body must be aching
Entwine must I mine sandalwood mortals
In you to ease the crammings
Oh, I must smear you with my
Embalming paste of turmeric
With rose water therapeutic

O king of my pious realm
Reign here with sovereignty
You and I make us of us
This clandestine rendezvous
Transform us into an incandescent
Ethereal being not to be unwind!

 **Mary Ann Cabuyao Abril** was born in Manila, Philippines in 1969 and has over 15 years of experience in teaching Social Sciences in the College of Teacher Education at the Batangas State University – Malvar Campus. She rose from the ranks to spearhead programs and developmental plans for quality assurance as Director of Research, Extension, Planning, and Development and later as Dean of the College of Teacher Education. After over 13 years working abroad as a Human Resource Officer in a multicultural international consultancy company in Qatar, Dr. Abril rejoined the institution in February 2022 and is now the Head of the Quality Assurance Management Office. She was recently selected by the International Organization of Educators and Researchers, Inc. as one of the recipients of the "Most Outstanding Innovative Leader and Researcher Award" in December 2022. Focused on her commitment to excellence and service, Dr. Abril returns to her niche with positivity and the determination of making a difference. Receiving recognition for all her contributions not just in the academe but also while working abroad, Dr. Abril aspires to achieve more and be an inspiration to everyone.

On the Day We Meet

Let my name into your heart
Stamp my likeness onto your mind
Leave the sound of my laugh in your memory
Hold on to me in the midst of a chilly night.

Likewise, my beloved
Thy glimpse is a delight to my soul
Your embrace appeases my troubles
You are my life and my home.

Through the march of time
With your hand in mine
We turn our odds and woes
Into laughter and light and hope.

Looking up, I pray—
Let our life be lengthened further
For us to be together, in worship and prayer
Till that fated day, Abba Father!

Das Schnäppchen (The Bargain)
Berthold Woltz, c.1896

 **Glenda M. Dimaano** is a Filipino associate professor for the undergraduate and graduate teacher education programs at Batangas State University JPLPC-Malvar Campus. As an educator, she is primarily interested in the pedagogy of social sciences and gender development across basic and tertiary education levels that focuses on teachers and students' capacity to engage in dynamic curricular opportunities and experiences within the context of teaching and learning process. She is also interested in writing any literary piece.

I'll Look After You

Let me tend to your wounded heart.
and teach you to fly.
Allow me to grip your hand softly.
and bid your tears farewell.

I'll show you the way to tomorrow's brightness.
and away from unnecessary rain,
Because all I desire at this moment
is to witness your latest smile.

I'll perform all of my original songs for you.
till you fall asleep in my arms,
and till then, I'll keep you warm and secure.
Your face is stroked by the sunlight.

Let me take you to the top of the mountain.
and I'll allow you to reach for the stars.
to bring to your attention the power I perceive
as I focus on your eyes.

As we kiss, I'll demonstrate what love means to you.
and the joy it produces.
You'll float like a butterfly once more.
possessing attractive wings.

I'll do all of this so you can see.
Our destinies are linked.
You're the unintended valuable diamond
To find, I've waited a while.

Together, the ground and the sky brought us together.
They understood we both belong.
pleasant phrases and sweet notes to one another
give each song some life.

So come, my lovely, fly with me.
We need to go past the past.
You can keep me, and I'll keep you.
At long last, we are at home.

Sophie Jupillat Posey is a French-Venezuelan poet who wrote a poem about spring in the 4th grade and started a mystery series a year later. She's been hooked on creating stories ever since. She studied writing and music at Rollins College and has had numerous short stories and poetry published in literary magazines since 2014. She enjoys reading and writing anything from science fiction and fantasy, to paranormal and mystery novels. When she isn't writing, she is composing music, creating albums, and teaching students in France. She can be reached on Twitter, Facebook, and her website. She is the author of *The Four Suitors* and the short story collection *The Inside Out Worlds: Visions of Strange.*

Lightning

Striates of lightning across the sky, they fork and dance wildly,
Blinding lines of white in the field of vision,
Forking on and on in the darkly purple sky,
The sky like an overripe fruit,
Ready to implode and explode with unlimited passion.
Lightning streaking excitedly across the heavens,
White filigrees of light flashing from cable thick to sliver thin
Tendrils of energy, like my thoughts and love for you,
Across the distance, across time, across the limits of the earth and sky.
Thunder rumbling in the distance, swelling and receding like the tide,
Reaching out to you, to the ears of your body and soul.
I listen to the thunder as it grumbles through the heavens,
Energy feeding in on itself, crystallized in the thousand lightning bolts,
Rushing madly through the skies, 3,700 miles a second,
To your fiery lightning heart, great expanse of mind,
And rich and crackling soul, like mine.
Lightning striating across the sky, forking and dancing wildly,
They are us as we find each other over and over again,
And they embody our love, streaks of energy traveling in and out
Of our souls at 3,700 miles a second, greater than the twenty breaths
We breathe per minute, greater and faster than body organs,
We are lightning, defying time and space.

Traveler

He lies on his side, back turned to me, half his back in shadow, and his lower hips in light,
A soft muted honey light that curves around his hips,
Highlighting the smooth texture of his skin, unblemished white
And vulnerable like the underside of a conch,
Skin cool and soft to the touch.
He is tired, the traveler, and he sleeps deeply, right arm outstretched,
Hand slightly unfurled, as if he had been holding someone's hand before falling to sleep.
His back undulates gently as his breath rises and falls rises and falls.
As I perch over him, his eyelids stay firmly shut,
Dark lashes small butterflies at rest,
The laughter lines around and under his eyes
Barely visible in the light.
His thick well-shaped eyebrows giving him a determined look
Even in the relaxed softness of sleep,
Yes, this traveler has been through rough times and good times,
I can see it in the topography of his skin,
Even if he hadn't spoken to me.
I reach out to stroke his face, stroke his scruff that darkens so well
The perimeter around his lips and chin and neck
But I do not want to break the spell.
His scruff is a palette of short hairs; dark brown, gray, white and red,
Like blades of grass just pushing through the earth of his skin,

All in various stages of birth, life and decay, like his
Memories, dreams and hopes and fears.
His hair spreads out behind him in a toffee mane of
    waves,
Some filaments of white and red meandering away,
Like the silt and minerals on the side of a riverbed;
Rich and natural, perfect for a traveler to touch,
    appreciate,
All the elements of life. I marvel at this traveler,
Whose path has crossed mine, our lives touching,
Our respective streams mingling and joining to pool into
    the ocean
Of travel and destination.
At last we have found each other, and I wonder
How this weary and determined traveler found his way to
    me
And I to him, both bedraggled but hopeful,
And at the marvel of nature, how our topographies match
    and differ,
He, the mountain to my river, I, the ocean to his desert,
He, the earth to my jungle, I, the ice to his arctic bank.
Cultivating the coal, the rust, the marble, and the silver of
Life; like the dark brown, gray, white and red hairs around
    his mouth.
Traveler, we are part of Nature, and I will protect you
From the earthquakes and the volcanos,
The tsunamis and the typhoons,
The hurricanes and the tornados,
The fires and the floods,
I will protect you and keep you safe
In the womb, the cave of Lascaux, where my love for you
    is painted

On the ancient walls, in the most primitive form of
 expression and art there is.
Us. Nature. Where our love will travel from 15000 BC to
 the infinite AD.
I will protect you and keep you safe, in my arms,
In the arms of peaceful sleep as we lie together
As you lie on your side, back turned to me, half your back
 in shadow, and your lower hips in light,
A soft muted honey light that curves around your hips,
Highlighting the smooth texture of your skin, unblemished
 white
And vulnerable like the underside of a conch,
Skin cool and soft to the touch.
And I turn out the light, but though my eyes can't see,
The layers of gray, indigo and black darkness can't hide
 from me
That you are there, here, now, with me.

Love Letters in Poetic Verse

Traveler on a Country Road
Jacob Ernst Marcus, 1813

**Amanda Valerie Judd** returned to school to earn her Associates of Fine Arts degree in Creative Writing from Normandale Community College after a 25-year career as a paralegal. She is currently attending Southern New Hampshire University for her Bachelors of Fine Arts degree in Creative Writing - Poetry. In 2020, she won the Patsy Lea Core Prize for Poetry. In 2021, her poem, "My Only Label" was nominated for Best of the Net 2021. In 2022, she won the St. Joseph County Library Spill the Ink Poetry Contest (Adult Division). Her work has been published or is forthcoming in *PAN-O-PLY Magazine*, *MockingOwl Roost*, *Trouvaille Review*, *Prospectus*, and *Talking Stick 31*.

Visit her at www.amandavjudd.com.

Doug

I knew I loved you
in that first second or two.
Tangled in your gaze,
my heart set ablaze.

Holding my breath that you feel the same,
lest I perish in these flames.
That smile and quiet bravado
hiding more than I could ever know.

You forever changed my life
when you asked me to be your wife.
In that first glance, I found love so true;
lucky for me, you did too!

**Christine M. Du Bois** is a cultural anthropologist with three published books: one on immigration, policing, and race relations, and two on how humans grow, trade, and use soybeans. Her poems appear in a dozen anthologies and online magazines, including *BourgeonOnline.com*, the blog of *Prospectus* magazine, *PonderSavant.com*, the *CAW Anthology*, *Pif Magazine*, *Central Texas Writers and Beyond 2021*, *Open Door Magazine*, *Tell Tale Inklings*, *Valiant Scribe's Vultures & Doves*, *Words for the Earth* – A Poetry Project of the Red Penguin Press, the *BeZine*, *Visitant literary magazine*, *Last Leaves* magazine, in two anthologies from the Ravens Quoth Press, and in *The Dope Fiend Daily*. Poems are forthcoming in *Psychological Perspectives* and the *Canary Literary Magazine*. She has had a short story published in the *Ecstasy* issue of *Libretto Magazine*. An avid birdwatcher and eco-volunteer, she's also a precinct Judge of Elections near Philadelphia.

French Toast

Warm cushion of questions
asking my tongue
about silk and sweetness
and lips—
pillows of lostness
in the sugar of yes,
union in the instant
of tasting
no need to add honey:
you already are.

Ken Gosse usually writes short, rhymed verse using whimsy, and humor in traditional meters. First published in *First Literary Review –East* in November 2016, since then in *The Offbeat*, *Pure Slush*, *Parody*, *Home Planet News Online*, *Sparks of Calliope*, and others. He was raised in the Chicago, Illinois suburbs. Now retired, he and his wife have lived in Mesa, Arizona for over twenty years.

Sweet Pen of Youth

If ever a poem's fully true,
may it be what I write of you;
your starlight sparkling ever bright
keeps blinding me throughout the night
while all day long your fleeting song
o'er whelms my sense of right and wrong—
that tune, your soul which mesmerized,
those words, your flesh which tantalized—
enrapt by mists which hid my fears,
awash in dew poured from my tears.

My mind in peril on a sea
of turbulence, where hope for me
seemed shipwrecked 'fore its christening;
trembling, swaying, my heart listening
for the faintest ringing bell,
the promise telling all is well
and storm-tossed agonies relieved
by what I wished for yet believed
would never be within my grasp;
that tender hand I'll never clasp.

So many words I write in vain
keep bursting forth from deepest pain
but fail to touch that lacey hem
so near, nor rubied diadem
that floats o'er beauty of your grace,
your warmth, your heart, your gentle face.
Yet it's beyond my greatest skill
to write or speak or even will
to come to life, thence touch the truth
of wonders of your precious youth.

Advice from a Father to His Daughter and her Beau

If You Plan to Marry a Man

If your mother was here,
I'm sure she'd draw near
with advice wise and nice,
very sweet to your ear.
But since I'm alone,
I'd best not use the phone—
if I call I would bawl
for the loss that we've known.

If you should plan
to marry a man,
it behooves you to find
the best one you can,
who'll walk close beside you
to help you and guide you
and when he's above you,
will pull you, not shove you.

He'll be a swell dad
and not a foul cad,
a washer and cooker,
perhaps a good looker
who'll earn enough bread
with a true, level head,
and won't only play in
but help make your bed.

He'll laugh along with you
and carry a tithue
to dry your damp eye
'neath a dark, cloudy sky.
A wonderful guy
whose life isn't a lie;
who'll be honest and true
when he says, "I love you."

Then, if you find
that your heart's on his mind
and you've come to learn, too,
that his heart's within you,
please marry this man—
set a date for your plan—
for there's reason to hope
that he's not just a dope.

If You Hope to Twirl a Girl

If you hope to twirl a girl,
don't feed her lines which make her hurl.
Your bawdy stories just might dock her—
in that case, why not just sock her?
Never assume a locker room
is where she's searching for a groom.

Even if she plays the tart
and fills a phrase with gutter art,
still seek and find her gentler heart
for sometimes we all play a part—
most often just to get along—
for we're all hoping to belong
while deep within we shun what's wrong.

Don't forget to add some polish:
clean your act and don't demolish
work begun in hopeful fun—
you're in to win and not to stun.
Prepare for a long-distance run,
for this is how dear hearts are won.

Learn what she wants; fulfill each need.
Accomplish this by word and deed.
Forsooth, in truth, this game we're in,
when played just right, is when both win.

Consider, too, that if you marry,
sometimes she'll be quite contrary,
oft' your fiercest adversary,
reaping for her cemetery!
So take care: be kind but wary—
there's a pit in every cherry.

Yet, with tender, loving care
each pit may blossom in Spring's air,
its petals falling on your bed
reminding you of why you wed.

If she's the girl you'd like to twirl,
her body, mind, and heart will whirl
when comes the season
you're the reason
that she chooses to unfurl.

Lovers
Auguste Renoir, 1875

**Bill Cushing** was born into a Navy family and lived in several states as well as the Virgin Islands and Puerto Rico before moving to California. Because of his experience as a marine electrician prior to beginning studies at the University of Central Florida, classmates dubbed him the "blue collar poet." He earned a Master of Fine Arts in writing from Goddard College in Vermont. He recently retired after more than 20 years of teaching in Los Angeles area colleges and resides in Glendale with his wife and their son.

Bill's work has been published in print and online by various journals and anthologies, including both volumes of the award-winning *Stories of Music*. Bill was honored as one of the Top Ten L. A. Poets in 2017, was named one of the "poets to watch" in 2018, and has previously had work nominated for a Pushcart Prize and Best of the Net.

Bill's volume of poetry, *A Former Life*, won a Kops-Featherling International Book Award. His chapbook *Music Speaks* won the San Gabriel Valley Poetry Festival chapbook award and a New York City Book Award. His latest chapbook, *. . . this just in. . .,* incorporates a number of ekphrastic poems.

Morning

Is
my favorite time of day:

Waking to an aroma of mangoes,
your scent;
feeling the weightlessness
of curly hair;
I can hear the easy
rise of breath;
a sculpted
cheek and chin
rest on
my right shoulder
while the thumb and
forefinger of my left palm
lay flat, forming
a "v" along
a smooth cheek.

Then, in a manner that would humble
Helen of Troy herself,
you rise,
languid and liquid,
and the lunar glow
of your cool body
moves into the light, casting
a crescent shadow
around your breast, your hips.

Then your face
turns toward me
and a smile spreads to
greet the day.

Then,
I rise with you.

Previously published in *A Former Life* (Finishing Line Press, 2019)

A Suadela's Shardoma

I feel the
edge of her nails as
her hand strokes
my arm. Her
inked dragonfly brings me to
the art of longing.

Enticing
me from the corner
of the bed,
one bare and
bended leg beckons, and I
lightly kiss her thigh.

First published in *Otherwise Engaged*

**Liwanag C. Rubico** is a Language Instructor and Program Chairperson of Bachelor in Elementary Education in the College of Teacher Education at Batangas State University JPLPC-Malvar, Batangas, Philippines. She holds a Bachelor's Degree in Secondary Education major in English at University of Makati and acquired her degree of Master in Teaching the English Language, at De la Salle University-Manila. Likewise, she was designated as the Head of the Office of Student Publication and adviser of The Laser, the official campus paper of the university from 2017 until the present time. She manages the office and spearheads the campus journalists in producing editions such as literary folio, magazine, newsletter, tabloid, and broadsheet. She brings prestige and honor to the university through winning in various competitions held in the regional and national level of campus journalism. Moreso, she had published literary genres about love, war, friendship, and topics dealing on pandemic issues. She has been serving the academe for 30 years and is an enthusiast in teaching literature, language, and grammar courses. In addition, she has published and has presented research papers that dealt on educational pedagogy in national and international research fora.

The End of Exodus

I've mastered the art of slipping away
from fingertips before daybreak
one step
carefully after the other

pray the floorboard won't creak
pray I land on a soft mulch and a flowerbed,
If I jump out the window pray my heart isn't beating loud enough
I don't stay long so my heart doesn't have to be hurt

it's easy to be around the fence for so long,
I've forgotten what it feels like to stay

quiet feels like uncharted territory

when I've been
around bustling crowds and getting lost

when I've had years' worth of favorite songs, ruined and named
constellations

there
is no other choice but to flee
but you,
your love tells me a different story—

here is where
I'll keep your hands in mine till daybreak and more.
here is where I wouldn't have to worry if my heart
screams your name

because I know, from any ocean to a meadow, yours will
always be screaming mine
here is where walking on tiptoes is never an option
darling, the way you waltzed into my heart
made it seems like twirling
dancing is the only way
to move about in our love

here is where I cherish the quiet time

misfortune has been hot on my heels and this love is
where i am finally
catching my breath.

here is where I'd give you all my favorite songs.
I have found a love greater than keeping these tunes to
myself
here is where I will name the stars after you
I am claiming all the light
of the night time as mine
let the gods be furious—I have found my place.

here is where I wouldn't try to leave unscathed.
a place where we meet against all haste
here is where I wouldn't try to leave
the Haven of love where you and I live.

 **Dr. Teejay D. Panganiban** is an instructor for the undergraduate teacher education programs teaching major and professional courses at Batangas State University, The National Engineering University, JPLPC-Malvar. At present, he handles various designations such as the Program Chairperson for the Bachelor in Physical Education, Head of the Culture and Arts, Adviser of Melophiles Band, Adviser of Human Kinetics Society, and Head Coach for Sepaktakraw Team of the university.

His passion in sports, music, and arts was translated into research articles where he has published his works in *Scopus Indexed Journals*, CHED accredited journal and international peer-reviewed journal with sterling reputation. Also, his research papers were presented in national and international research fora and he served as adviser and panel member for student researches in the college.

He believes in the value of arming physical education students with practical, lifelong, and health skills, which cross over subject matter in order to develop a character for a positive personal, family, and community life.

Leap of Faith

You were quite a stranger but not a different face
Found myself staring, my heart is at race
There's this feeling inside of me that I cannot understand
Until you approached me and held my hand

Still in shock, don't know what to do
Am I supposed to laugh or just smile at you?
You hand me my book that fell on the floor
May you also hand me my heart for I think it's already yours

There are things that I cannot tell you
I am not a coward, just don't want some issue
Our world is very different, I am aware
You live in comfort while I live in despair

There is still hope inside of me, I won't deny
I pray that one day under the same sky
You and me will be together
But now I will just pray and work harder

Treasured Love:
A Tapestry of Joy and Pain

Love is a feeling deep and true
A bond that grows and strengthens as we do
It lifts us up and makes us whole
A love that makes our hearts unfold

It's a fire that burns bright and hot
A love that can never be forgot
It's patient, kind, and full of grace
A love that we can't help but embrace

It's a journey that we travel hand in hand
A love that weaves its way throughout the land
It's a tapestry of joy and pain
A love that we'll cherish forever, through sun and rain

So hold on tight and never let go
For this love is worth more than gold
Embrace it fully, with all your might
For this love is a treasure, a beautiful sight

Tristian and Isolde with the Potion
John William Waterhouse, c.1916

Michael H. San Miguel is an instructor for the undergraduate teacher education programs at Batangas State University TNEU JPLPC-Malvar. He is also a research-based faculty member who is trained in quantitative, qualitative, and mixed methodologies of research in the same university. He has published research articles on Physical Education and Sports pedagogy and educational management in CHED accredited journal and international peer-reviewed journal with sterling reputation. Currently, he is working as the Head for office of Sports Development Program, and Head Coach for the Athletics team of the Batangas State University system.

Forever My Anchor

From the moment I laid eyes on you,
I knew that you were the one for me.
Your smile, your laugh, your touch,
All of it fills my heart with joy.

You are the light that guides me through the darkness,
The rock that anchors me in rough seas.
With you by my side, I feel invincible.

I love you more with each passing day,
And I thank my lucky stars that you came my way.
I promise to cherish and adore you,
For all the days of my life.

Forever yours

**Moe Phillips** is a native New Yorker and a believer in all things magical. She credits her Irish ancestry for her love of words and wonder. Over thirty of Moe's poems and essays have appeared in anthologies and magazines for adults and children. Whether Moe is delving into the world of Fairy folklore, silly poems, or essays that honor daily living, they all contain her imagistic style of storytelling. Moe's latest poetry endeavor is a tall tale series of audio stories entitled *The Feisty Beast.* She has created films for award winning poets - Naomi Shihab Nye, Rebecca Kai Dotlich, and Georgia Heard as well as several shorts of her own for New York City's beloved Wild Bird Fund. Moe is a member of the SCBWI - NYC chapter. Moe was recently the first poet featured on The Dirigible Balloon's website-Moe Phillips. A wonderful children's poetry website out of Yorkshire, England.

Lovers on the Brink

Locked together in eternity,
The lovers stood on the brink
Holding hands and wondering
will their vessel sail or sink?

Recalling their promised pledge
he said *"Together let's grow old.*
We can brave the icy waters.
Trust our tale has not been told."

"I'm not the maid you married.
My bones can't take the fall!"
"In my arms, I promise you,
You'll feel no pain at all"

The lovers leapt into the breach,
Plunged through the midnight sea
Fearing nothing in that void,
For their love would always be

Robert Burns and Highland Mary
Nathaniel Currier, 1846

 **Marianne Tefft** is a poet, lyricist, and voiceover artist who daylights as a Montessori teacher on the Dutch Caribbean island of Sint Maarten. Her poems appear in print and online journals and anthologies in the United States, Canada, India, Serbia, United Kingdom, and Sint Maarten. She is the author of the poetry collections *Full Moon Fire: Spoken Songs of Love* (Tellwell Talent, June 2022) and *Moonchild: Poems for Moon Lovers* (December 2022).

Her work is available on Facebook (Marianne Tefft - Poet & Wordsmith)
https://www.facebook.com/MarianneTefftPoetWordsmith
and YouTube (Marianne Tefft)
https://www.youtube.com/channel/UCALiRAX7idctDYEZOUhy-eQ

You Have Never Seen the Ocean

Is it true, love
You have never seen the ocean
You come from an ancient land
Locked away from the sea
Where the first hunters roamed
In waist-high grass
And climbed for days
To the tops of cloud-wreathed mountains
Now you stand on the edge of a new land
Birthed from ancient volcanic hips
Cradled in the waves
Where the first fishers dove through spindrift
To forage plains of turtle grass
Is it true, love
You have never seen the ocean
Run beside her with languid steps
Out-racing footprints indelible
Only for the time between the crests
That endlessly erase the shore
Seen the Sun tease the horizon
Strewing rubies and diamonds
That dissolve into the sea
With a flash of phosphorescent green
Is it true, love
You have never seen the ocean
Plunged beneath the waves
To bathe in a timeless caress

And leaped through the surface
Your smile effervescent
As you raise your chin
Your mighty locks flinging
Prismatic water-fans
Into the luminous moonset
Is it true, love
You have never seen the ocean
Here you will write windswept poems
Breathing in the salty exhalations
Of our restless mother
By night the stars will crown my hair
Candelabrum around my head
Shining on our table in the sand
Where we dine on each other
Long and lingering feast
As Aldebaran and Rigel arc across the sky
And the waves kiss our bare feet
Is it true, love
You have never seen the ocean

Jone MacCulloch inspires minds young and old with her poetry, photography, and art. Her work is driven by Naomi Shihab Nye's quote, "See poetry everywhere." Jone describes her work as spare and guided by her Irish and Scottish roots. Her passion for poetry is seen in her involvement with the children's literature poetry community where she participates in Poetry Friday on her website, Jone Rush MacCulloch.

Post retirement as a teacher-librarian, Jone guest teaches in Southwest Washington. Children think she is a book fairy because she wears rainbow tinsel in her hair.

Her poems, photography, and art have been published online and in several journals, including *The Silver Birch Press*, *Spark: Art from Writing and Writing From Art*, and *The Poeming Pigeon, Volume 12*. Her most recent children's poem is in *What is A Friend*. 2022 edited by Sylvia Vardell and Janet Wong, Pomelo Publishing. She has also won local awards for photography and poetry.

Jone is a member of the Society of Children's Book Writers and Illustrators, and Haiku Society of America.

Jone lives in Oregon where the coast, rain, the changing seasons and skies are her muse.

You can find her on Twitter @JoneMac53 and on Instagram @jonerushmacculloch.

Night Mysteries

My body seeks the mysteries of night
Ocean, wind gusts: a symphony
Candle flickers, silhouettes dance
Faint whispers, secret caresses

Breaths syncopate to crashing waves
My body seeks the mysteries of night
Smell of salt, taste of vanilla
After the candlewick burns low

Lunar light glows through the window
Your arm drapes, pulling me closer
My body seeks the mysteries of night
Missing puzzle pieces now in place

Sleepy, we spoon as the tide ebbs
Gibbous moon fades into the sea
Ocean, wind gusts: a symphony
My soul seeks the mysteries of night

 **Carol Edwards** is a northern California native transplanted to southern Arizona. She lives and works in relative seclusion with her books, plants, and pets (+ husband). She grew up reading fantasy and classic literature, climbing trees, and acquiring frequent grass stains. She enjoys a coffee addiction and raising her succulent army. Her work has most recently appeared in anthologies from Southern Arizona Press, The Ravens Quoth Press, and White Stag Publishing, and in *Space & Time* issue #142. Her debut poetry collection, *The World Eats Love*, is scheduled for publication by Raven Quote Press in Q1 2023.

Blinded

Moon's light on ocean waves
All my life enchanted me -
Until you stood near and gazed out.
Now I see nothing.

My eyes reflect just you
Moonlight in still water.
Rain makes ripples come -
A gift of a hundred you's.

Moonlight's kiss is but tissue
paper when laid next to
the feather of your touch.
You reach for me, and I grow wings.

The rain stops and the moon sets.
I leave the ocean again.
All the magic stays there with you.
None of it returns with me.

Love, Observed

Love sounds like the silent bedroom door,
whisper footsteps in and out,
use a phone's glow
to miss meeting metal dog bowl with toe.

Love smells like acrid bleach and mild dish soap
notes of lavender and pine,
floors scrubbed clean,
soft cotton billowed by a cool breeze.

Love feels like iced water on a hot day,
Hands massaging knots away,
quiet embrace
on days when life stings, tears down our face.

Love tastes like morning buttered rosemary bread,
sweet-tart strawberries,
squeezed pineapple juice,
bitter chocolate from beans brewed.

Love looks like the back hunched in work and pain,
persistent warring
the same demons each day,
sacrifice of time and youth for gray.

Love is in the staying through the worst
long past the "how it should be,"
deep soul groans long-suffering
under a barrage of blasphemy.

Love Letters in Poetic Verse

Southern Arizona Press

Previous 2022 anthologies from Southern Arizona Press

Love Letters in Poetic Verse

The Stars and Moon in the Evening Sky is a collection of 120 poetic works crafted by 65 poets from across the globe inspired by the universe around us.

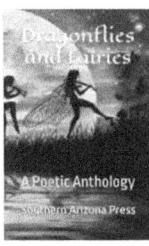

Dragonflies and Fairies is a collection of 72 poetic works crafted by 34 poets from across the globe celebrating the magical and mystical creatures of folklore.

Ghostly Ghouls and Haunted Happenings is a collection of 129 poetic works crafted by 46 poets from across the globe inspired by ghosts, ghouls, and things that go bump in the night.

The Poppy: A Symbol of Remembrance examines the history of the poppy as a flower of remembrance, over 80 poems and lyrics written by World War One poets between 1912 and 1925, and 79 poems written by 21st Century poets from around the globe in remembrance of the fallen heroes from all war of the last century.

The Wonders of Winter is a collection of 120 poetic works crafted by 50 poets from across the globe that celebrate the winter season.

Upcoming 2023 anthologies from Southern Arizona Press

Castles and Courtyards – An anthology from 21st Century poetic bards celebrating the medieval life of kings, courts, peasants, and troubadours. Coming in early April 2023.

A Midsummer Night's Dream – An anthology of poems celebrating the plot lines of Shakespeare's famous comedy: Weddings, the Woodland, the Realm of Fairyland, Under the Light of the Moon, along with poems about the summer solstice (Litha) and any other fond memories of summers past. Coming in early June 2023.

Beyond the Sand and Sea – A gathering of poetic works inspired by the sea, seashore, lighthouses, or anything else associated with life on or near the sea. Coming in early August 2023.

The Children's Book of Bedtime Verse – A collection of poetic works appropriate for reading to children at bedtime. Coming in early October 2023.

Home for the Holidays – A holiday anthology of poetic works celebrating the gathering of family during the fall and winter holidays. Coming in early December 2023.

Poets interested in submitting works for upcoming anthologies are asked to check out our Current Submissions page at: http://www.southernarizonapress.com/current-submissions/ for more information about each anthology and our process for submission.

New independent releases from Southern Arizona Press

The **Midnite Cab Company** (by cj fletcher) never existed, yet, it is always present. "Driver 51" never was, but, always is. The dilemmas faced by both are not 100% true, yet, they are also faced by many of us on a daily basis. Driver 51 was never a hero, never a savior, yet he bears witness to the twists and turns of the events portrayed in this volume. The best lies contain a kernel of truth, and the truth many times begins from a lie. Throw caution to the wind, step into the rabbit hole, and decide for yourself.

https://www.amazon.com/MidNite-Cab-Company-cj-fletcher/dp/B0BKRZX3VF

Look Behind You is a collections of Elaine Reardon's poems which are elegiac in the unfolding of life in its multitudinous everydayness. Here you find her immigrant parents' pasts expressing themselves in the everyday habits and rituals of "old country" and their assimilation into an American present that both distorts and keeps them alive as well as allowing Reardon to express them in delightful engaging cadences.

https://www.amazon.com/Look-Behind-You-immigration-assimilation/dp/B0BKLDPBVZ

The overarching theme of Elaine Reardon's poetry chapbook, **The Heart is a Nursery for Hope**, is life, in all its quirkiness, from small moments in the day to life changing events. Whatever the heart holds can nourish and transform.

https://www.amazon.com/Heart-Nursery-Hope-Elaine-Reardon/dp/1537561111

Southern Arizona Press

A Heroic Crown and Other Sonnets is a collection of 110 sonnets written by Paul Gilliland. It includes traditional Italian, English, Spenserian, Terza Rima, and Couplet sonnets; the more obscure Kyrielle, Vondel, Pushkin, Jeffrey's, and Brisban sonnets; the newer Eramonean, DOnnet, Reflective, and Form 28 sonnets, and his own creations of the Fourteener, Drabble, Golden, and Inverted Trochaic sonnets. The collection is topped off with the inclusion of his epic 15 stanza "A Soldier's Heroic Crown Sonnet."

https://www.amazon.com/dp/1960038001

Wishbone in a Lightning Jar - "What would I write in a message to my future self?" Is the enigmatic question Sharon Harmon's poetry asks. Each of these poems portrays a window into the landscape of the heart, exploring the whimsy as well as the sorrow it holds. Wishbone in a Lightning Jar is a poetic journey that illuminates and celebrates the poignant moments of a deeply felt life.

https://www.amazon.com/dp/1960038044

Grass in Green - "Whatever Tasneem Hossain depicts becomes vital to exploring meaning of life in our otherwise occupied consciousness. And her diction makes the subjects, be it myriad facets of nature, or our tears, smiles and sighs, come so alive that her poetry, in effect, verges on a visual art. Her poems inspire emotions and are crafted in soulful words. Both stir the hearts of many to pause, think and feel a renewed urge for life. A stellar example of how simple words can craft profound feelings into a beautiful piece of poetry."

https://www.amazon.com/Grass-Green-Collected-Tasneem-Hossain/dp/1960038060

In this, his second book of poetry, Thomas Zampino imparts flashes of intimacy, intensity, and inevitableness. At its core **synchronicity** can be read as a love story. One not only existing between lovers, but one that also reveals how synchronicity - seemingly unconnected moments of "co-incidences" - lovingly shaped a life fully lived. A lifetime of poetry observed, told without pretense or presumption.

https://www.amazon.com/synchronicity-Thomas-Zampino/dp/1960038028

Through artfully crafted language, internationally acclaimed poet Norbert Góra explores his unique perspective on our current condition and evokes profound beauty amid the dark realities of the modern world. His work adeptly expounds on the fatal flaws of society while maintaining an uncommon and indispensable sense of hope. In **Deadlines**, Góra offers a deeply insightful meditation on the human experience as we interact with the physical world, the constructs we have created, and our fellow denizens herein"

https://www.amazon.com/Deadlines-Collected-Poems-Norbert-G%C3%B3ra/dp/1960038052

Individuals interested in working with Southern Arizona Press to bring their books to print are asked to review our publishing services at:

https://www.southernarizonapress.com/publish-with-us/

Southern Arizona Press

Published works by our featured contributors

Imagined Indecencies is Rp Verlaine's third book. Poetry that is Profusely Illustrated with color photos taken by Verlaine of models and friends who posed for him. The poems are haiku, Seneru, sonnets, and one-line poems. A notable change from previous books is there are several free verse poems as well. All the poems have been published before in Literary Journals, Magazines, Newspapers, and websites. They have been published in Japan, Africa, Wales, Scotland and of course Verlaine's native America.

https://www.amazon.com/Imagined-Indecencies-Rp-Verlaine/dp/145663867X

Incidental Moments invites the reader to come along on a literary journey featuring poignant and powerful poems interspersed with generous helpings of humor. Mark Fleisher's narratives weave tales spanning a broad array of subjects while his use of imagery paints pictures both abstract and realistic.

https://www.amazon.com/Incidental-Moments-New-Selected-Poems/dp/1949652181

Love Poems for Michael by Joan McNerney
Many reflect on New England with autumn foliage and fierce winters. However, four seasons do include bursting springs and boiling summers. Love is its own season, its own country, its own domain. Let's explore love up north during spring and summer.

https://www.amazon.com/Love-Poems-Michael-Joan-McNerney/dp/9388319656
https://www.cyberwit.net/publications/1602

At Work by Joan McNerney explores everyday workers. It is unique because each worker, either female or male, receives their own page. These are snapshots of people who are either content with or made unhappy by their daily circumstances. Reading this book is an exploration of human nature at its core.

https://www.amazon.com/At-Work-Joan-McNerney/dp/8182537835

https://www.cyberwit.net/publications/1759

The Muse in Miniature by Joan McNerney
There is no doubt this poet very aptly traverses an immense range of emotion and experience. Here we find poetry's passion and powerful imagination in rich abundance.

https://www.amazon.com/Muse-Miniature-Joan-McNerney/dp/9389074509

https://www.cyberwit.net/publications/1262

Love Letters in Poetic Verse

The poems of Tasneem Hossain's **Floating Feathers** are an outcome of the spiraling moments of her emotional outbursts. The title poem is a confession of the poetic thoughts floating and falling into her lap. *Let's Walk Together, You and I* deals with old age agonies and pains of becoming senile. Human emotions, social justice, kindness towards humanity and transience of life are some of the themes of her poetry. At the end there is a collection of haiku poems.

https://forms.gle/4JdcJi792ZSZS63R7

Tasneem Hossain's book **Split and Splice** is a compilation of some of the writer's articles published in different newspapers dealing with historical events and interesting facts about different issues, some are about acquiring good habits for a peaceful and successful life, some discuss ways of improving lifestyles and overall well-being having relevance to day to day life. The different aspects of life will help readers to become more conscious of life and the world surrounding them.

https://forms.gle/4JdcJi792ZSZS63R7

Poetry to Tasneem Hossain is an ever-flowing river reflecting all that surrounds us. **The Pearl Necklace** is a lyrical journey of sensitivity and contemplation through life in its different colors and shades. The title poem is about unfulfilled true love. *The Invisible Cord* is a celebration of mother's love. *Agony* is a cry for social justice. The last poem *The Lighthouse* ends with an aspiration to make our existence more meaningful. The essence of her poems is the beauty of nature and human life.

https://forms.gle/4JdcJi792ZSZS63R7

Sometimes compact, sometimes expansive, the 28 poems in **Women Who Were Warned** emanate from adolescence and other liminal spaces, considering girlhood and contemporary womanhood – and the ways both are fraught with the pleasures and limits of embodiment.

https://www.amazon.com/Women-Were-Warned-LindaAnn-LoSchiavo/dp/B0B28D58G8

Apperception is a new poetry book about the excessive dreaming process we experienced during the pandemic. Dreaming often takes us back to our childhood memories and wishes as we deal with our confinement. In the book, the dreaming poet vanquishes her foreboding dreams that intuit the pandemic by realising that the lockdown made us all more vulnerable.

https://www.amazon.co.uk/s?k=apperception+by+emily+bilman&crid=39HMYC6DETGYI

Wolves Don't Knock is a psychological drama/thriller, along with suspense, mystery, romance, and family relationships. Suitable for mature teens and up. Twenty-two-year-old Miranda escapes from her abductor and the wolves that have tormented her soul for six long years. She returns to her childhood home where her mother, Sharon, caring for Miranda's son, Kevin, has feared for her daughter's fate. Uncertainty and distrust taint the first year after Miranda's return. Miranda and Sharon hide secrets they dare not reveal while constantly wondering when Miranda's kidnapper will reappear. Can mother and daughter bury their demons and repair their strained relationship? Can Miranda bond with the baby she never knew and find the love she so desperately wants? Will Kevin's father play a role? Will Sharon find the answers she needs to recover from her own troubled past?

https://www.amazon.com/Wolves-Dont-Knock-C-MacKenzie/dp/1927529387/

Mister Wolfe tells the story of Paul Wolvescoten. This is an explicit book, with scenes and language suitable for 18+. Mister Wolfe is dark; the author calls it a "darkly dark" book, but she can't help how Paul turned out, for he dictated her words, forcing her fingers to sweep across the keyboard—telling HIS story. Perhaps he got caught up in madness. Sometimes everyone does, right? Now that Paul has had his say, Pauline (his sister) is clamouring to tell her side. She holds the key to unlocking the families' secrets—or most of them—for she isn't privy to everything.

https://www.amazon.com/Mister-Wolfe-C-MacKenzie/dp/1927529689/

Against the Waves – Selected Poems is a collection of R.K.Singh's 66 poems, including two long, experimental haiku-tanka-haiku sequences, 'God Too Awaits Light' (2017) and 'Silence: A White Distrust' (2021). Most of the poems have also already appeared in both online and print journals, with or without translation in Romanian, Japanese, Spanish, Arabic, French, Crimean Tatar, Italian, and other languages.

https://www.amazon.in/Against-Waves-Ram-Krishna-Singh/dp/B0953RT4Y1

She by Ram Krishna Singh is a collection of 57 haiku, celebrating woman that makes man complete. It effectively presents various facets of a woman's life, from sex to divinity, that impacts man everywhere. The poet's latest book of haiku personal and yet universal in image and meaning. It is available free for reading.

https://www.calameo.com/books/00355283198a950fde5f8

Donna Kelly's ***Cop Eyes*** is a fast-paced suspense novel about an Illinois public defender, Cheney Manning, whose police officer husband is killed in the line of duty. When Cheney's former client is charged with the first-degree murder of her husband, Cheney undertakes her own dangerous and reckless investigation in order to pursue the truth about what really happened on the night her husband was killed.

https://www.amazon.com/Cop-Eyes-Donna-Kelly/dp/B09NN55PYV

Love Letters in Poetic Verse

In Sophie Jupillat Posey's debut novel, **The Four Suitors**, quick-witted and confident, Princess Laetitia of Avaritia always gets what she wants—until her 17th nameday ball. The King and Queen, believing marriage will rein in their daughter's rebellious nature, surprise the Princess with not one, but four suitors: a philosopher, an astronomer, an artist, and a necromancer.

https://www.amazon.com/Four-Suitors-Sophie-Jupillat-Posey-ebook/dp/B07W62533W

Along with other twisted tales, **The Inside Out Worlds** stretches the bounds of our reality.
With an undercurrent of magic and subversion in worlds like our own - emerges a fascinating, twisted, and completely captivating collection of ten stories. A millennia-old vampire desperate to find a way to feed on humans who've exchanged their flesh for robotic bodies. A little girl who can see the embodiment of Death himself. An antisocial loner has prophetic dreams of an apocalyptic flood. A new social media platform that can leech life right out of you.

https://www.amazon.com/Inside-Out-Worlds-Visions-Strange-ebook/dp/B09S3YWWBS

Offerings to Selene takes the reader on a magical journey of lunar splendor. Through illustrative poetic storytelling, Sophie Jupillat Posey masterfully paints the moon in all of her vibrant facets: the nurturer, the sacred one, the seeker of vengeance, the beaming entity that reigns supreme over Earth and all of her dwellers... However, this celestial voyage goes beyond Lady Selene herself; it is also a transformative trek into the psyche. Within its luminous pages, this chapbook urges each reader to commune with the moon on a soul level.

https://www.amazon.com/Offerings-Selene-Sophie-Jupillat-Posey-ebook/dp/B0BFRVZDLD

James Thomas Fletcher has provided poetry for every reader. **Bibliophile** has three sections. Poems about family fill "The Tie that Binds." Poetry about art is the theme of "A Thousand Words." The book ends with a section of humorous poems, "Flights of Fancy."

https://www.amazon.com/gp/product/B09V8F1NP1

James Thomas Fletcher's work is often about nature but here he speaks out on politics, history, religion, and ecology in a collection of eclectic musings. He writes of discovering an arrowhead and of discovering patience. Of stretched friendships and lost loves. Of unity and division, JFK and FDR, of November 3 and January 6, and about reading and writing poetry.

https://www.amazon.com/gp/product/B09GMVYLFQ

Additional titles by James Thomas Fletcher, all available on Amazon

Wild Seeds: Contemporary Idylls
The Visible Spectrum of Desire: An Interstellar Love Story
War: New and Selected Poems
The Covid Chronicles: Poetry from the Pandemic
Roses for the Canyon
Mercury & Moonlight
Émigré: Poems from Another Land
In a Burst of Recycled Electrons
Cairn
Poems from Terra
Nature: New and Selected Poems
Love: New and Selected Poems
Death: New and Selected Poems
A Pentateuch Of Poetry: The Complete Collection of the First Five Books
Rue Gît-le-Cœur

Love Letters in Poetic Verse

After nearly 40 years as a corporate and property tax attorney in NYC, Thomas Zampino's poems just about popped into existence at the **Precise Moment** when they could no longer be held back. This is a broad selection of mostly simple observations about life, faith, and meaning as seen through the eyes of someone who was profoundly touched by the world around him long before he realized it. Influenced by American poet Billy Collins and English poet David Whyte, these poems are a reflection of the aging - and hopefully the maturing - process in real time.

https://www.blurb.com/b/10812828-precise-moment-pb

Finding My Heart in Love and Loss are poems full of a remarkable diversity of poetic thought, therefore it will have a wide appeal to all readers of poetry books. These poems never fail to stimulate our imagination, because the poet very aptly succeeds in providing 'addition of strangeness to beauty.' The poems are quite lyrical and appeal to the innermost heart and mind of the readers. Here we find lyrical intensity and visionary strength of the poet.

https://www.amazon.com/Finding-My-Heart-Love-Loss/dp/9395224630

Marianne Tefft's poetry collection is inspired by the phases of the Moon - waxing, full, waning, and new – **Full Moon Fire** traces the journey of love from bright to bittersweet and back again. Born under the Caribbean sky, these 40 "spoken songs" are romantic poems that speak to every heart that has ever loved under the full Moon.

https://www.amazon.com/Full-Moon-Fire-Spoken-Songs/dp/0228876451

A poetry collection bathed in Caribbean moonlight, **MOONCHILD** by Marianne Tefft, celebrates winter, spring, summer, and autumn under the full Moon. With 40 romantic poems for Moon lovers, MOONCHILD speaks from the heart to all those who love in every season under the bright night sky.

https://www.amazon.com/Moonchild-Poems-Lovers-Marianne-Tefft/dp/0228882230

Cai Quirk's **Transcendence: Queer Restoryation** invites readers into a world where distinctions of gender, time, and place become fluid and flexible. Binary ways of seeing the world will not simply disappear — we must actively replace them. 38 self-portrait photographs and six mythic tales explore paths beyond supposed binaries, creating new stories that empower, inspire, and heal. The book comes out this March with Skylark Editions (skylarkeditions.org).

The Last Polar Bear on Earth - `From motherhood to Joan Baez, internet dating to the inside of an MRI machine, Rhian Elizabeth's moving and often witty poems cover a range of subjects. ... While this is a collection about nights out and trips to Madame Tussauds, of tenderness and joy, of being young, at its heart is a group of poems about Multiple Sclerosis - the interactions with doctors, the symptoms, the rubbish benefits system. Brave and unflinchingly honest, these are poems of the greatest importance and achievement.' - Jonathan Edwards

https://www.amazon.co.uk/dp/1912109476?ref_=cm_sw_r_apan_dp_FJ2F5W69AHSES7CT0SCM

It is Mark Twain who said, "write what you know." Doug Croft goes deeper. He shares what he feels. A non-academic writer, Croft embraces himself as a "simple poet." His poetry has been described as patriotic, minimalistic, and pointed. ***Exposed Roots*** explores Croft's personal love of nature along with family roots. He bridges patriotism and social justice. The themes of religion and love take us to final messages of hope and happiness.

https://www.amazon.com/Exposed-Roots-Doug-Croft/dp/1681114909

Thanks Dear God (Without God's Grace, Life is Meaningless) by S Afrose reflects each and every part of life, as per the perception of Author. Every word is expressed heartfully and showing her gratitude to dear God .Let the world know, the magic of her Poetry. Here or there, each word will touch any of the sight of your dear life. But don't take anything personally. It's all about the emotional flow of love for Poetry, which helps to revive the beautiful life on earth, as God's Boon.

https://www.amazon.in/dp/9354469612?ref

Poetic Essence by S Afrose. It's a great pleasure to share my emotions with the magic of ink. They come as my friends. They want to show up with their pride. If there's anything, which may differ from your thought, then never mind. Don't take anything personally. I love to write poems. Poetry holds me as beloved.

https://www.amazon.com/dp/621470392X

Reflection of Mind by S Afrose - it's such a poetic canvas, where mind has sketched its dreamy thoughts, using divine colours. All are sparkling as usual, everywhere. Thoughts in motion have reflected, as parts of the Beautiful Life. Those perceptions, dreams, dance every time, by the source of inking spirits.

https://www.ukiyoto.com/product-page/reflection-of-mind